All in one Digital Marketing: Strategy, Analytics and Research for Business Dummies

A digital marketing book using blogging, Facebook, Twitter, Google and Amazon and many more in 60 Days

Hemanta Saikia

Green Booker Publishing

Copyright © 2016 Green Booker Publishing

All rights reserved.

ISBN: 1539847004
ISBN-13: 978-1539847007

DEDICATION

To my Parents, wife Emi Kalita and other family members.

CONTENTS

Chapter:1 Introduction to Digital Marketing	1
Chapter: 2 Success Platform	10
Chapter: 3 Website Optimization for Digital Marketing	21
Chapter: 4 Social Media Marketing in Broad	38
Chapter: 5 Facebook for Business Marketing	74
Chapter: 6 E-Mail Marketing	92
Chapter 7 Blogging Marketing	118
Chapter: 8 Digital Marketing Research	154

ACKNOWLEDGMENTS

I would also like to give my special thanks to my family whose patient love enabled me to complete this work. I extend due respect and gratitude to all those who helps and co-operations will be valuable and precious for all time to come before me.

CHAPTER:1
INTRODUCTION TO DIGITAL MARKETING

Digital Marketing?

Digital marketing is the endorsement of a product or any service and brand or entire company using entirely virtual means such as social media such as Facebook, Twitter, LinkedIn, paid media such as Google Adwords, email marketing, email newsletters or search engine optimizations. Another very important element of digital marketing is that it should be centered on a strategy of being able to monitor your results; so social media posts are not just shaped and drawn up but they can be observed, monitored and watched and people are engaging intermittently for providing a conversion.

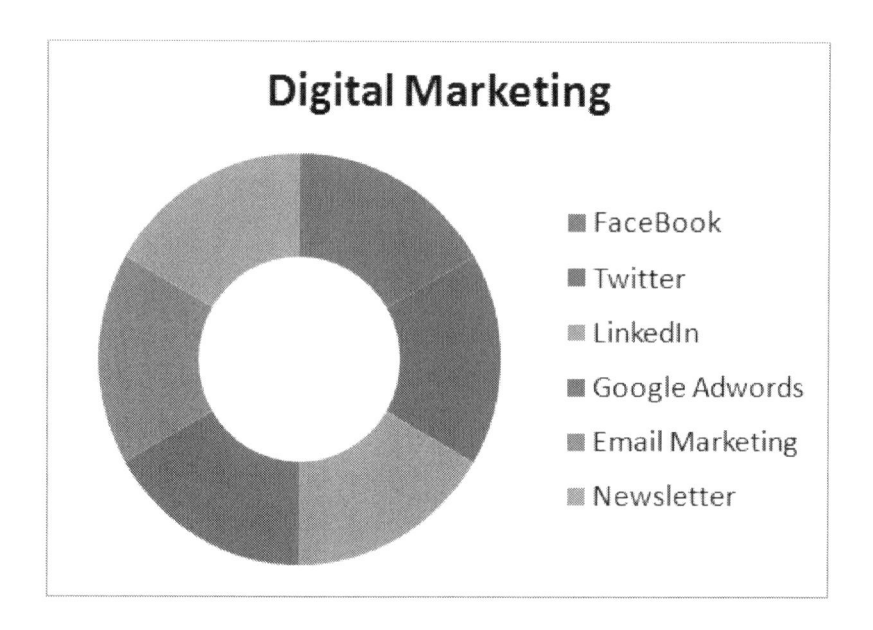

Digital Marketing

- FaceBook
- Twitter
- LinkedIn
- Google Adwords
- Email Marketing
- Newsletter

In other words, digital marketing is the marketing of products or services using Digital Medias to accomplish consumers. Here, the key purpose is to endorse brands through various forms of digital media channels. However, the digital media is any digital tools that you can use in any *digital marketing strategy; somewhat a website, content management system, an e-commerce site, includes search engine optimization, as well as your contents, videos, pictures, graphic design*, and lastly, social networks such as *social media*, etc. the other ways your sharing the content. In other way, digital marketing is the efficient and effective way of communication that valued through digital media so that your customers understand the value of wants which they find out more efficient. This implies the people i.e. your customers may actually understand exactly what are you selling? What you offer them? Why you are using digital media.

Benefits of Digital Media:

The Key benefit of digital media are

1. Cost Effective;
2. Easy to learn and manage
3. It is creative
4. Increase sale
5. Easy to diagnosis

  Digital media help you many ways; firstly it's incredibly cost-effective, sometimes you free for your marketing strategy. Secondly it is easy to learn and manage. It is creative and easy to manage and helps to sale. There are many ideas of what digital marketing means? Some think it means having a website or advertising or getting your site found top in the search engines results. Digital marketing ties together the creative and systematic aspects of the web with strategies. This includes designing and enlargement, consciousness building, communication, association, customer service, sales and business analytics etc. Let's discuss each item systematically:

Consciousness:

  You can have the better goods or services but people must knows what this is? Digital marketing is finding out ways to build awareness.

Communication:

  Communication is about information distribution or simply education; communicating who you are, whom you serve etc.

Connection:

  The heart of digital marketing is connection. This is where we get people to be acquainted with us to like us and to belief us.

Service:

  Service one of the most overlooked items of the digital

marketing. This is where public may get frequently put questions, answered; may have a good experience shopping with you, or getting to pages of your website or simply being found in the search engines may be considered good service.

Sales:

In the last item of the creative aspect are sales. All of these aspects i.e. awareness, communication, connection, service etc come together to help boost sales and digital marketing include using of these medias like digital advertising, working on search engine marketing (SEM) or search engine optimization (SEO) and also includes the email marketing, social media marketing, content marketing using web analytics, digital public relations, mobile marketing and user experience optimization and combination these options.

Meaning of Digital Marketing:

According to Wikipedia, Digital marketing is just like a sunshade for the marketing of goods or services using digital know-how, for instance internet together with mobile phones, exhibits advertising and any other digital means. Digital marketing has stretched since the 1990s and has altered the way of branding and marketing technologies. Digital marketing campaigns are now a day's becoming more widespread, as digital stand are gradually more included into marketing plans, and as people use more digital devices instead of going to traditional physical shops. It includes, search engine marketing (SEM), search engine optimization (SEO), influencer marketing, content marketing, campaign marketing, content automation, e-commerce marketing, social media optimization, social media marketing, display advertising, e-mail marketing, ebooks and games, and other forms of digital media platform. It also enlarged to other channels, such as mobile phones (SMS & MMS) etc. Digital marketing is also referred to internet marketing, online marketing, or web marketing etc. In the USA the term online marketing is still widespread; in Italy it is termed as web marketing and in the UK and worldwide as a whole the term digital marketing is a common term. Traditional marketing has shifted from linear marketing platforms such as one-way communication to a value exchange model where there is two-way mutual side platform and benefits are sharing between service provider and consumer as well. Now marketing platforms are more non-linear and free & elegant and both one to one and one-to-many and many-to-one. Digital marketing and identify areas to improve as well as leverage new opportunities is where success lies.

Digital marketing works not only to help in acquiring customers as well as used as a power hub support on repeat sales and acquisition and retention. Truly, meaning of marketing means maximizing associations. We must also address the art and science of digital marketing. There is a close heart relationship in marketing and sale that makes marketing matter. There are few touch points to make a sale. Touch points can be a referral web search, a social media, a press release, getting email or seeing an online advertizing. Email marketing another most powerful ways to continually connected with accessible customers as well as enlist present customers. Online public relations are another area within a cover where you could become your individual media manager to increase your credibility and visibility. Social media one of the key component today and biggest pieces of the online marketing runner today which is going to include everything from a blog to facebook to Twitter, the linkedin etc. Even comparison shopping sites and online advertising where you paid to be found and can be on display ads like Banner. Advertisements or in search engine as or even email newsletters and lastly the most valuable piece of marketing real estate is the website itself.

Digital marketing get help to receive perspective customers to know like and trust. The web is change per minutes and the way we work, communicate, spend time or spend money. The chief online promotion distinctions are that it is 24/7. That means even when you are sleeping online marketing is up and working for you. The worldwide visibility can open your business to a global market. Another distinction is the ability to capture sales and leads online directly and you can reach a much targeted market so even if you have products or services in certain pieces. You can affordably make pieces by being found to people who want specifically what you are offering.

In summary these help to maximize your customer

acquisition and retention by saving your time and money and human resources. Now, consumers are more empowered and expect information at the click of their fingertips. Therefore, a strong digital marketing presence can give you a huge competitive advantage.

Digital marketing Vs Traditional Marketing:

In this world of technology, traditional media and digital marketing they are becoming important tools for how we behave professionally and how we share a business tools. What differentiates traditional marketing and digital marketing is actually very simple. Traditional marketing will costs very high; but it also very relevant and necessary. The biggest distinguishing factor between them is digital marketing gives you answers immediately and is tractable; you know what's working and not right away. Traditional marketing doesn't really give you answers immediately; that does not mean that you are not getting response or much of a return on your investment. There is a unique balance between the two. How much digital marketing should be incorporated into a brand? What separates these two is the brand's vision and mission; what the brand wants to achieve based on these?

Distinguishing both, we can come up with the appropriate marketing plan of digital or traditional or a mix of both. In today's market, we know that a mix of both traditional and digital is what gets the best return. The main benefits and downsides of traditional marketing are:

Benefits of Traditional Marketing	Downside to Traditional Marketing
You can easily reach your target local audience.	Print or radio advertisements can be very costly.
The materials can be kept.	Results on this marketing strategy cannot easily be measured
It's easy to understand.	It is somewhat complicated

The Key benefits of modern digital marketing are:

Benefits of Digital Marketing
You can target a local audience, but also an international one
Your audience can choose how they want to receive your content
Interaction with your audience is possible
Digital marketing is cost-efficient
Data and results are easily recorded
Level playing field
Real time results
Brand Development

Scope of the Book:

Today, time has changed and people want information instantly at the click of their fingertips. They are gathering to the web to find products, services and information. In this book will first create a foundation by defining how digital marketing works and identifying its dissimilarities and components. Planning and online marketing strategy will be also discussed which determine your target audience and measuring the results of your marketing efforts. Preparation and build a website is crucial for the accomplishment of your online marketing strategy. From creating a site map and building a wireframe to selecting a domain and hosting company will explore the necessary steps for getting your site up and running. For there, we will tackle the key elements for establishing a web presence including making, convincing, online content in the form of articles, social media posts, and online press releases and even email newsletters. Prominent website content is able to only take you so far without having an audience; so we will cover how to reach and develop your viewers through victorious search engine marketing including search engine optimization and paid in local search. There is a requirement of harnessing the power of social media including facebook, twitter and linkedin in addition to blogging to stay your viewers updated, well-versed and engaged and finally will try analyze online advertising in addition to email marketing to assist or gain precious sales and exposure.

CHAPTER: 2
SUCCESS PLATFORM

Platform for Success:

There is a grand speech *"**We do not plan to fail, we fail to plan**"*. If we wish to build a house without a blueprint it will be towards failure. You need to approach online marketing with a plan which creates a healthy foundation. Therefore, strategy should be formulated first and execution in next. Here, digital marketing helps to build a website from the ground up or optimize online marketing foundation that already exists. There are several success steps that must be considered as planning points in these processes. The five access points to consider for Digital marketing preparation are: ***Credibility, Usability, Visibility, Sellability and Scalability***.

Diagram: Planning (center) surrounded by Credibility, Usability, Visibility, Sellability, Scalability

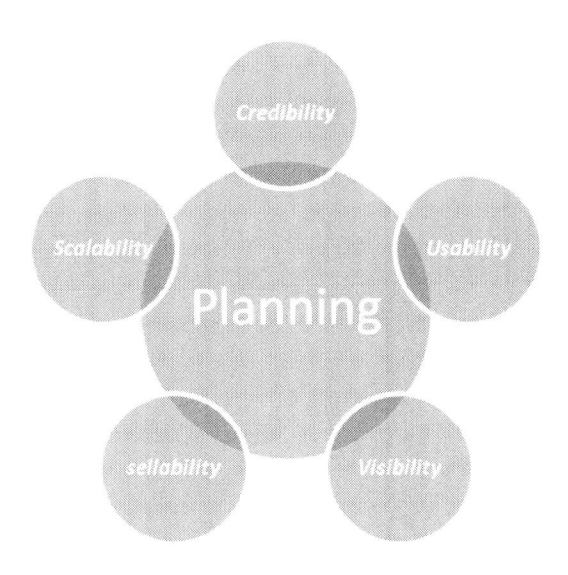

Credibility:

Credibility is the impression we make online executed on web site, to our content, belongs, videos, PR, social media or views. We never have a second chance to make a great first impression and building trust in online marketing is the key focal point. Every effort should be made to create credibility of a website or a brand or company.

Usability:

Usability refers to how well people can use your online marketing efforts. Marketing work needs to be user-friendly. It comes from appropriate and professional design, site architecture, clear navigation, call to action, email, content and even social media marketing.

Visibility:

Visibility is critical in build your digital marketing plans. We can propose the best goods and services but if no one knows about them, what's the value of such efforts? Visibility can come from a number of marketing channels including natural or organic search, advertising, social media, or email or you may have a healthy visibility options of planning ensuring marketing mix. Having that idea of what visibility channels will be used is serious to imagine about as you plan. This visibility options may require space on your web pages; may be integrated into necessitate additional budgeting, design, or take some technological setup.

Sellability:

Sellability is a critical marketing planning platform and this is how well you sell the value of your organization products and services. People need to understand why you or your organizations are worth working with? This can come through and videos, testimonials, press releases, taglines and photos. Other way, sellability means communicating and educating your value and online marketing, planning process which will ensure that your value points are won't into site pages and but also in overall online marketing work.

Scalability:

When we engage in recreation of credibility, usability, visibility and salability, we reap the benefit of scalability. Digital marketing efforts can last a lifetime on the web building or compounding over time. Digital marketing scalability like a good stock or small investments made consistently over time can grow to support an organization's overall web presence and marketing.

Measuring the proper Market size:

Now you have already seen the five success steps that work together to make your online marketing worthy. The next critical step is target the market, ideal customer and their needs and problems? Understanding your targeted market will ensure that they are served from the time to time for promotions, arrive on your site and avail their entire user experience. You only have a few seconds to make a meaningful impression. With the competition, a click or two away linking with your perfect customer by accepting is so important. When you think about online marketing, keep in mind that we desire to draw supreme prospects. Repeatedly, we get wrapped up in warning traffic which affects a lot. The key is to spotlight on drawing and linking with people who really matter. So, we don't waste our time, energy and wealth with public who are not the best prospects. Distribute your marketing time wisely by first identifying the people you really want in your customer base.

With digital marketing, we need to create, execute ideas and then monitor our execution. Measurement helps in deciding how to best use your time and energy and monetary resources. Success metric that both qualitative and quantitative; for example qualitative success metrics could be things like branding, credibility building, sustaining future dealing objectives and generating PR consideration. Quantitative success metrics can be things that are mathematically measurable: links or web inquiries, number of email sign-ups, traffic and sales. When you are planning your online marketing foundation, always plan to have web statistics built-in from get-going. One of the big distinctions of online marketing is its traceability. Many success online marketers like to say if you can measure it you can manage it. This can only happen if web figures are building into the system of your website. There are a lot of different web analytics tools; one of the most widely used services called Google analytics. Web analytics help to measure traffic volume, submitting sources of traffic &

quantitative objective like sales, email sign-ups, conversion rate and even referring search keywords.

Website Orientation for Digital Marketing:

Site Map:

The map or outline is the vital approach for online marketing. To successfully build a solid website a website map must be documented before new design or optimization began. This will insure good marketing behavior and key components which must be included and will also give you or your web designer clear expectations from designing. The planning stage helps to remove additional and unnecessary redesign or additional programming work. Think the website map like building a house. You need to identify what rooms of the house will need to be build.

We can look an example of simple website http://www.apple.com/in/ of Apple company website in India. Here, the site map is as simple as a documented above that has a list of the website pages in the order that they will appear in the navigation like this text version or a site map can also be more visual where the pages are represented in map forms.

Mac → iPad → iPhone → Watch

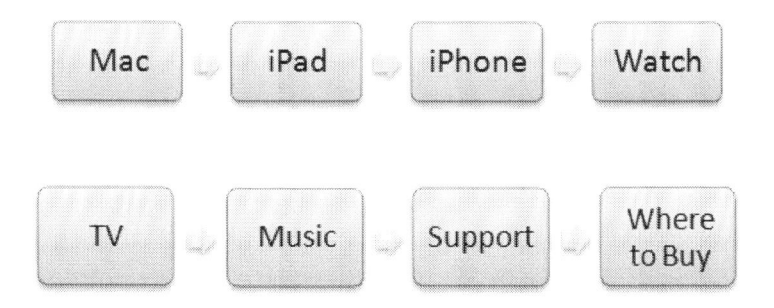

TV → Music → Support → Where to Buy

Whether you are designing your own website, designing for an organization or managing a web design, this is a critical online marketing step as it insures that the site is built with all the important pages and in what order. There is a lot of work to do before pre-planning phase of a website which can be termed as strategy phase and next phase is execution i.e. application. In the planning process you may want to include pages from main navigation, sub navigation and even footer links. Since we have covered the mapping of a site, next we will move to define your site components.

Defining Website Components

Website components are the items owner want in the main rooms of your house or plan to include in online marketing widgets like Twitter, Facebook, YouTube or LinkedIn that users can click to build your email newsletter list a priority. You may want a sign-up box designed into your site.

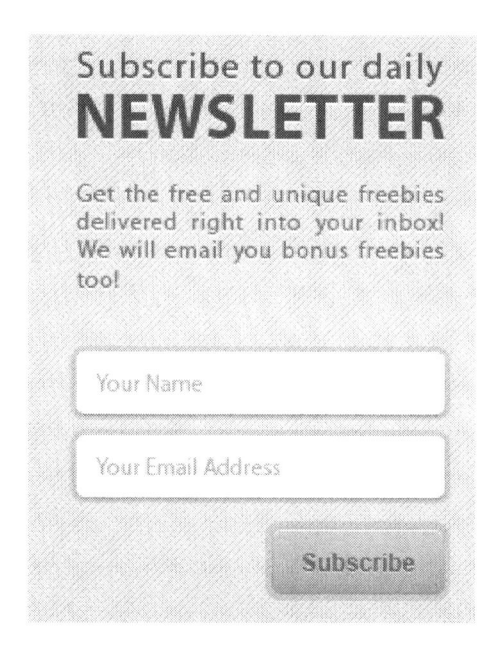

Here are some examples of online marketing site components. What you will see are things like get a free ebook; this is a button that helps promote action for someone that potentially would like a free ebook, things on the footer of a website like blogger, YouTube, Facebook, Privacy Policy, Copyright, little links that have small icons.

Let's not forget the email sign-up; you will see things like 'join your e-list to get news articles' etc. You don't have to design the components like you see here. You must have a clearly idea what components you want to includes in the design process.

Website wireframe

Website **wireframe** also recognized as a page representation or screen blueprint is an illustration guide that symbolized the very thin structure of a website. **Wireframes** are shaped for the idea of assembling the site elements to best achieve an exacting reason. The most valuable marketing lies in the small space & time in your computer monitor or for mobile sites. A site homepage and other critical pages of your website can be architected via wireframes, so that critical pages are visible and certain actions are encouraged by website visitors.

The website is your online marketing center. We can use the opportunity and you can't lose it. Website visitors need to be guided through site, once they get into it. Before design, work began as wireframe ensures that the placement of page navigation, order & site components all have a place. Wireframe is typically done in black and white to stay the center on mapping out where belongings will go on a page. For example CNN website can be visualized in term of Wireframe as:

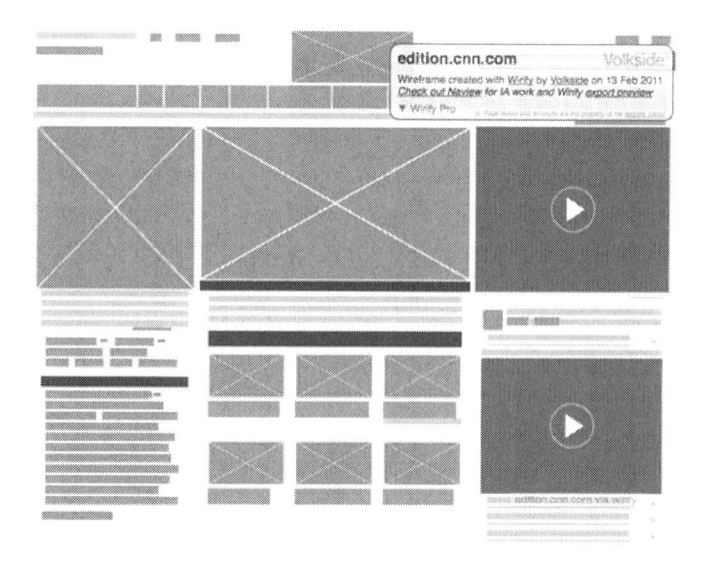

In a sample CNN wireframe the goal was to show the placement of navigation like Home Page, Video, News, World News, Asian News as well as where introductory copy and headlines would go. The purpose is more about architecture versus colors and text. This wire framing step helps by keeping the focus on getting approval on layout before coloring and designing. Web marketing and planning sometimes such that some text is used in lieu of real text during the wire framing process to show where text will go. Even if the text isn't ready for the site, wireframes can be designed with graphic tools and repeatedly they are only drafted out on a part of paper. Wireframes can be done with or without graphic tools. There is no one-size that fits all solution as tempting as it is to start designing sites. Successful website is not so much as the site, instead as the web solution. The elements critical for successes are clear architecture with wire framing process where you want your photos to go headlines, certain text, photos, call to actions things like social media widgets.

Framing Website Navigation:

The next necessary element is simple smart navigation. Wbsites having a clear plan of the order of pages like home, about us, services, blog, contact us that need to be planned out before. Call to actions things like may be a button or also simple words like learn more, a link into other pages of your website and components like email sign-ups, newsletter signup etc. If you want to augment, people signing up for newsletter required to be planned as part of the successful footstep process. Importantly, a booming site needs to serve up the aim of market and be focused on really offering them great customer service as a means indirectly towards sell. Having a successfully strategized site will support your overall online marketing efforts.

Designing Homepage of website:

The homepage is like the front door of a house. Homepage is a drawing room to make people feel comfortable and reinforced that they are where they are supposed to be; but also guides them to where you want them to go. We want our visitors to our sites but we have to get them through the site to a focus page or to our product page and smart homepage always fulfill the purpose of the site or company purposefully. Homepage planning is a lot easier when you first start with the website map which has a wireframe and then moving into formal design. You may architect homepage just like you would plan a space like a room or office. Remember site mapping, call to actions, mindful marketing messaging is also required so that homepage is clicks as a marketing support tool. The homepage must clearly communicate with your clients or customers or visitors. It must identify some basic questions? What you serve and whom you serve? This can be spiked through an interesting logo, bullet points, website text, photo or even video.

The homepage needs to draw attention of ideal visitors or customers accomplished with mindful messaging. A final point to leave into your website planning process is your online privacy policy. A privacy policy is in online marketing is most needed requirement. Privacy policy addresses how you use personally identifiable information such as cookies on your website. Privacy policy also discloses if you sell or rent contact information. You can get a web search for phrase like privacy policy to see examples of privacy policy. Best practices you can use free privacy policy generators online such as free privacy policy etc.

CHAPTER: 3
WEBSITE OPTIMIZATION FOR DIGITAL MARKETING

For building online marketing foundation, you need to build the website yourself or hiring an expert. There are three important points to discuss: **time, money and expertise.** You need to have the time to build your own websites. You may know how to build websites or have invested in a website platform that helps you to build its own. Being able to build a website and having the time to build a website can be two very different things. Even if you hire someone to create the website for you, you need time to prepare your budget and time to manage the project. This may require time in writing website contents copy, revealing design, revisions and gathering components, like photos or videos etc. The second component is money and funds are required to hire people; if not, the decision on how to proceed may be determined by this point alone. The last point is expertise that has power to tackle your own website management problems. If you do not hiring a professional, you may not get the job done on time and on budget. Web designer or web developer may have the expertise required to get the job done right. But choosing of experts is based on time, money and goal of the company. This is an important decision that will help you critically evaluate what works best for you or your organization.

Site Platforms:

The next step of building a website is to decide in what platform is suitable for building a website. Those building the site from the ground up, you may be wondering about all the different platforms like Dreamweaver or content management systems also called CMS like Joomla, Drupal and Wordpress. In today's world making and managing websites is easier than ever and you may explore several options. You need to decide what to use; We need to analyze online reviews and look at sample sites. Here there are two big decision points when looking at website platforms. Ask yourself how important it is to self managed. CMS is that you have the ability to make a lot of your own website. CMS platform is based on what we know? How to work in or when our webmaster may give us return? So we can create content without any help. The second point to be sure about is how search ready your site is or that platform is? You website needs to be search engine friendly and schema.org friendly so that search engines can easily locate them and easily make visible in search results.

Along with platforms, Domain names are important to get a handle on whether your site is are ready to have a site live or are building one from the ground up. Generally you use same domain names for brand protection, search engine optimization and for online marketing campaigns. If you have a website working with already, be sure to find out right domain for the site, if you know all the domains your organization may own or secured extensions of existing names besides the.com, .io, .net,.org and.info. For brand protection you may want to secure those just of the competition.

You buy website addresses with your company name and if your company name is long, you may also choose something shorter for ease-of-use. A Business may use a shorter version that may be easier for customers to type when emailing or to put on business cards. Shorter domain can always redirect the longer URL reducing someone a little typing time. Sometimes you may want to protect misspellings of a company forename if the name can be commonly misspelled. Domain names can also be selected to support search engine optimization. Some organizations choose domains that have descriptive search phrases and then and use them to help in searches. Be sure if you have a domain name that you know you have from long time; you buy it for at least 5 to 10 years versus renewing annually. This can show your seriousness to that URL which search engines may affect into their search engine result pages.

     Once you have a domain name selected, you need to have website hosting in place. You may want to webmasters to see if they have a recommended solution. Here are some questions to ask: Do you have a small site? Or a large site with a lot of necessary room for files, images or hosting your own videos? Or is it okay to pay less for a shared server? Can your videos come from third-party video sites like YouTube? Do you need a dedicated server for more guaranteed uptime? Sometime lower-priced hosting package are minimize costs whether you are building a new website for optimizing an accessible site. Make sure find a hosting solution that works best for your needs to impact the speed of your site as well as its uptime.

Websites do not run themselves; the more you learn about digital, the more you will understand that there will be a need for periodic website updates and additions optimizations and new technology integration with website analytics. Keep records of the list of domains you own, how long it will end, your domain company logins, your hosting records, FTP access for your website, email system logins, access your logo files, login and password, web analytics login and even social media logins. You never know when you may need these for online marketing management. As important as it is to have a robust website and consider programming your website to be mobile friendly or build a dedicated mobile website. A mobile site is architected differently than a traditional website to accommodate the small space on the mobile screen. Some person may even come up with an idea for creative mobile apps to add to the online marketing mix.

Content Marketing

Content is anything that can be shared to tell your story. Content Marketing is the tools of media you created to share your brand's story online. Content marketing is about contents in the form video, audio, text, images etc. It is not a new concept, rather it is mainly used in news papers, journals, radio, TV etc; the only change is the platforms in modern times. When people want to buy a home, restaurant or anything else, they go to internet and search for items and pick up item that they like the most. That is the importance of good content and people like that item which was equipped with good content in the form of video, audio, images, text etc.

Content is an online marketing tool that can create a voice for an organization or individual. Content creates and sparks conversation. There is a great saying we learn to write by writing. Content can come from other people in your organization or you can hire expert writers to help you taking your ideas online. By understanding all the content marketing options, you can decide how to proceed strategically and write what you want or hire the workout. However you approach content marketing and social media is up to you but don't be afraid to be human. The social web is about being social; being yourself offer relevant entertaining and useful content.

Online content creation is a key to Digital Marketing success which carried jointly the achievement steps of credibility, usability, visibility, sellability and scalability'. Content marketing is defined as content that educate and empower web users. It is compelling online content that website visitors come to know, like and trust. Let's get into how to use content in a powerful online marketing asset. Content marketing includes each content that is website and emails, press releases, FAQ, frequently asked questions pages, shared on blogs and videos posted social media sites like Facebook, Twitter, and LinkedIn and even the things broadcasted and audio through podcasts. As you can see content for online marketing is more than just website text; whether you are a fresh organization, conventional organization or are solo business leader in the respective field.

Content Marketing in the form of Articles:

Publishing content in the form of articles on your website or an article sharing sites can multitask. It helps to build an awareness, communication, connection, service and selling tool. There are many article publishing places on the web. A web search for article marketing sites to see all of the content sharing options will help in this regard. It's great to know where you can publish but critical to know how to write articles that matter. Here are three writing tips:

1. Article need to be customized to serve the audience you want to attract; write as if he were speaking directly to your target customer.

2. Articles must be editorial-based; what this means is that it needs to be informative, pleasurable or idyllically a combination of both.

3. We need to remember to write articles that are too promotional. Article contents succeed as a marketing tool when it is written to empower readers; not to push products or services. Articles that

come across like commercials will not be well received. When you embrace the approach by: editing, marketing with an educational twist, articles are more likely to be read and articulated upon. Creating articles is only half of the fun sharing in online; the real marketing magic begins later. Articles can be shared on website or a article page or can be posted to your blog, option in email list and posted on article marketing sites. Just go online and search for all the sites you can post articles too; however, most of them are free. Another interesting idea of article marketing is that you have a shared common target market with an offer to guest write articles for them. This can help you to get visibility in other sites and reinforce your authority status. Once articles are live on the web they can also get socialized meaning shared via social media.

Social Media platform:

Content marketing has gone to a new level with the use of social media. Social media content can be everything from blog posts, Facebook post, tweets, LinkedIn post, videos and podcasts. Now a day's social media content like blogs are a big part of the marketing dilemma. When you are thinking of ways to add persuasive content to brand building and boosting business, remember the popularity of social media and social networking. People use these tools both personally and professionally. Search engines are fast in pick up social media contents where the visibility potential is pretty significant. When you move toward social media contents like blogging or video production; keeps in mind that the three 'Vs': **'Value', 'Values'** and **'Voice'**. Content on the blogger posted on a social site needs to have value to the reader; not be sales as propaganda about your company. Content can be educational, newsworthy, or can even be an interview with the customer. Content marketing via social media also needs to leave your values. Lastly, content and social media needs to be driven with the human voice. Unlike content like articles or press releases social media content is more conversational and we will discuss broadly later in this book.

Online Public Relation:

It is important to start thinking about the power of online public relations as part of your overall marketing strategy; it is saying that what you publish is so true when it comes to online PR. You can educate your potential customers about company news, your point of view on current events that relate to industry or split new invention or service information anything that is newsworthy. These days, we can afford to wait for journalists to create us as experts, we need to go to them with our news and also use online PR to educate our people with the same market adding concepts at marketing. Online press releases focus on the facts and it is a good exercise to write your own releases to share who, what, when, where, why, how and who cares to get the real heart of the story you are telling. Online press releases are sustained content creating way to share news, opinions, and events and keep the media, customers and even prospective customers, educated about the happenings in your organization. Think of press release creation is a way to spoon feed media news your point reviews and updates to help you to build your credibility visibility and sellability.

Email Content:

Content marketing can be work with planned messaging on your site or to your option in email list. When you are working on content marketing, you can say something especially in bullet points; in example an e-commerce website can be designed an email newsletter to send to their customers who've opted into the list from the sign-up box on their website. The email newsletter sign-up box promises registrants. The email newsletter will share news, articles and case studies. Content on the website for online marketing can include things like testimonials, frequently asked questions page and email content and the best part content marketing. The lives on the World Wide Web can multitask to support search engine marketing.

Study after study has shown that any social engagement is more visualized where there is any visual look; such as photos. Taking own photographs is easiest way to get a photo. However, there are some special sources from where you can get free photos for both commercial use and for personal use like istock.com, shutterstock.com, 500px.com, flickr.com etc. The best way to get photo is from own camera with the following ideas:

Photo Ideas:-
- Behind the scenes
- Production line
- Staff
- Product sketches
- Personal

For effective content creation, good and creative photo is required as messages or tweets are liked or shared most with having a photo in it.

Search Engine Marketing (SEM)

People mostly search for products and services are via search engines. Our sites need to be searched and found to attract new customers and to serve customers we are already had. Understanding the art and science of search engine marketing and its good practices can help you make little changes to acquire better online visibility results. Search engine marketing is defined as marketing through search engines. This can include efforts to improve organic listings, getting found in local search results, purchasing paid search, advertising or combination of search related activities. Think of search engine marketing also known by the ellipsis SEM as an umbrella term that includes all parts of search; organic, paid and local.

Search engine optimization (SEO):

Search engine optimization means making modifications to websites so that they have a superior possibility of come into view well in the organic or natural listings of search engines. The acronym for search engine optimization is SEO. SEO is not related to pay advertising. The results are based on an algorithm which means mathematical equations. They are unique per search engine. Despite the differences in search results per page every engine has a common goal to provide the best results as possible. Natural search results are driven by the engines algorithms, how well the site seems based on key phrases searched, the popularity of a website as well; there are many things to consider when tackling SEO; but the three main points set as a smart foundation or fundamentals: **architecture, content and linking**. Before we get into SEO building content & linking, we need to define the key phrases that you want to be searched and found on. Always plane your priority key phrases before any search optimizations are executed. Write down keywords that give details of your organization, products and services. There are billions of websites on the World Wide Web focusing on broad key phrases versus specific little keywords which give you a much better chance of attracting qualified searches result. Next step is to define priority SEO phrases is to find out those descriptive key phrases with the city or county they represent from. Certain organizations who only server certain market; there is no pint point for driving people to your site whom you can serve. Leaving interior descriptions can be smart next steps to attract perfect traffic if your industry is physically located, remember this equation. Business or service description plus location or region equals optimize marketing key frames. The power of targeting phrases to optimize pays to attract besieged search outcomes and carry the correct customers to your site. It is not the traffic you want to attract but also you want bring quality traffic in the form of right customer or right buyer or seller, reader etc. Create a list of perfect phrases that you like to be explored on; just remember that the phrases need to be specific to your business location; you should not used broad words that aren't specific to what you do. You can also really pull in those qualified searches which will be your compass for any future SEO work implements both natural and for paid search. The architectural structure of the website is very important to help a search engine. Site architecture includes the employ of URLs the code of site and even the cleanliness of your code. Blogs are becoming a brilliant piece of the SEO item because of the way they are architected. What is most important for SEO basics is to be mindful use of URLs and to have exclusive meta tags for each page of your website; for example website page can be set up his SEO or it could be SEO architected to have a priority key phrase or phrases that describe what the pages about. Most blogs automatically are making the title in the post & the key phrases in the URL. Next is your get your site architected for search success. You want to make sure the meta-tags of each page written in a way that helps describe each page. Meta tags may be termed as HTML code that can be altered either in the web system you manage or you can ask your webmaster to rearrange the meta tags for you. Architecturally talking, you can see how the URL on post has the keywords in the title. This was automatically or automatically done based on how the blogs codes were set up. Technically this is called a permanent link. Content comes up again as a power player in online marketing to support SEO. Content can be prepared with your priority key phrases where it is applicable to help attract searches on your blog and your website. Look seriously at website and copy page by page and find ways to put your key phrases and headlines and in the site copy itself. Use contents like what key phrases and blog posts especially in the titles and even as you write online articles and press releases. The much you understand SEO the much you will find creative ways to leave your phrases into site content, blog posts, articles and press releases. Content is a great way to educate and inform but when used traditionally for SEO you can get multitasking power out of it. The last piece of the SEO is linking search engines; look at how many links come from relevant sites the points your website but they also look at internal links on pages. You may request people to connect to your site if they are in balancing industries. You can also create your own linking power interpersonally with links between pages of your site.

Paid Search:

Online advertising can take your marketing to a new level when done tactically; it may not be necessary for every organization, there can come a time in the digital marketing process, when you make a decision to buy online ads to expedite, awareness, distribute your message, make linkage and support. Now and then, you have to spend money to make money. Let's look first at how search engine marketing can carry your overall online marketing goals. Search engine advertising is one of the most prominent places to buy digital advertising; search engine advertising when so many marketers online can make optimum advertising budgets because of its targeting power. You can target campaigns around optimal key phrases that people who are in the most key mindset and advertisers only pay when people click on their ads building the spending more resourceful. SEO is more likely to deliver people who are ready to buy ads that are targeted to phrases websites or geographic locations that you feel are the best match.

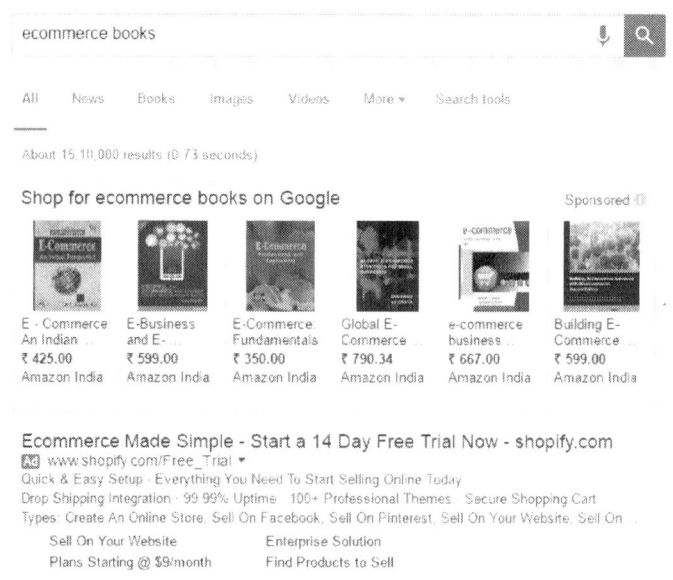

Ads can be in the search engines themselves or they can be in the other websites that of search engines partner. You can buy advertising on search engines like Google, Yahoo and Bing even on smaller search engines. Go to a different search engines and take a look at some of the ads out there to get the ideas.

Paid search is in online marketing help an organization in obtaining search visibility in the sponsored area of a search engine results page. Unlike natural organic search, paid search allows you to pay to be visible or advertisers bid on a per click basis to have their message appear. Marketers create their own message; can target their out by things like location and keywords searched and also have the ability to track how many populaces notice the listing; click on the catalog as well as even knowing the percentage of people who take an action like signing up. Just like we planned priority key phrases to target for natural search that same list can get we visited to become the key phrases you buy. For example when people are searching for the phrase "Web Hosting" there may be more attracted to seeing an ad with phrase that they search for in the paid search title or description.

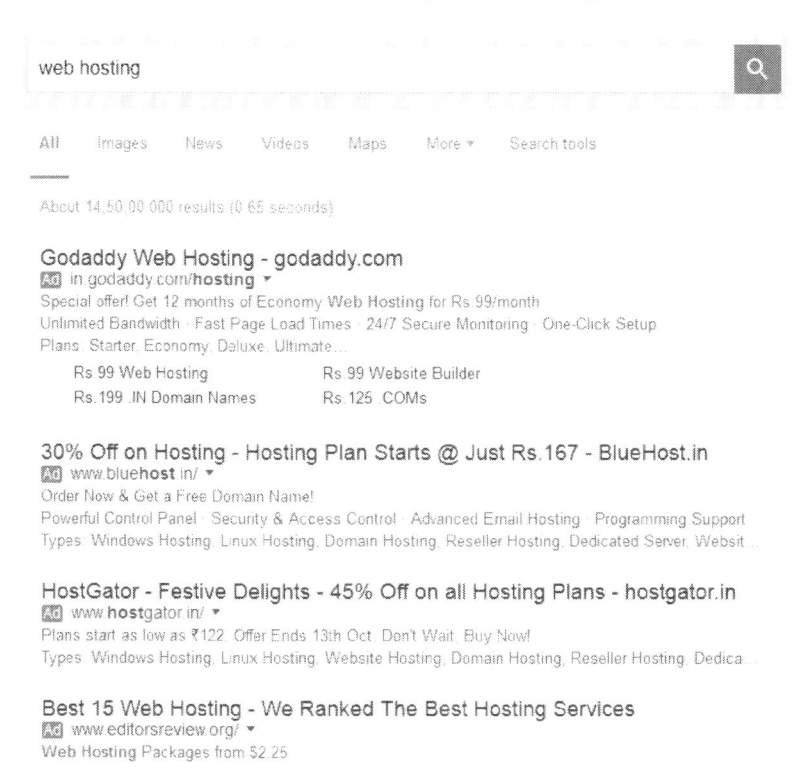

Having specific Ad copy that supports the phrase searched is a best practice; lastly, a tracking plan will need to be in place to measure advertising success. Success can be defined by traffic, calls in your organization to decide just to sure that money is spent and measured for return on investment.

Local Search Results:

One of the best parts about search engine marketing is that there are ways for local organizations to get searched and found in verticals; like local search. For example a business based in Delhi so what they can do is they can go to search engines like Google, Yahoo, Bing, and yellow pages can submit their business. To these vertical search engine specific to local search and the search engines may ask for verification either by calling a phone number or sending a postcard to the address with the piece of code in it but has to be typed in once you submit your business as long as you can verify that you are a business owner of the address that you work and you can get your site listed often for free simply by exploring local search engines. Local business owners can hit target by their advertising budget to have text ads appear in search results for local phrases that will listed only if you searches with their geographic key phrases in them like local newspaper sites, popular community sites and local resources that a certain geographic market visits. Local sites can be sold on a CPM CPC CPA or sponsorship basis. Search engine marketing is a powerful online marketing medium. Knowing the basics will help you use all of your marketing assets as best as you can to boost your visibility. Why do we care so much about search engine marketing is that if you are out of site you are out of mind?

Displaying Ads:

Display advertising is image-based way of promoting products and services online. Initially, they were referred to as banner ads. Display ads have evolved in many sizes since their first appearance on the web. Publisher's, also owners of websites: large and small website can sell space to interested advertisers. Advertisers can also seek out desires sites or have their ads appear on groups of websites. Their online advertising networks that represent a corporation of websites that one may also buy from there. Display ads range in size and technical capabilities. You can visit Google Adwords page to see all the display advertisement options. It is important to understand the pricing language as it relates to display advertising.

Impressions are defined as how many times an advertisement is viewed. This pricing metric came from traditional advertising like radio and television. Impressions are viewed as eyeballs. Cost per click (CPC) is based on the cost per click through click from the online advertisement to the advertiser's destination. Search Engine Advertising in the search engine sponsored links sections is most commonly sold on a cost per click basis or Pay per Click (PPC) basis. When Ads are purchased on a pay per click basis, there is no charge for impressions. Cost per Action (CPA) or cost per acquisition means payment by advertisers is made only of qualified actions such as clicks, sales or registrations occur etc. Ads also sold on a cost per lead CPL basis. Affiliate marketing is run on a CPA or CPL basis and has a distinct set of rules norms and management responsibilities. Some websites blogs are portals sell their advertising on a sponsorship basis; means that advertisers pay to appear in the website but there are no guarantees for impressions clicks or actions. Sponsorship permits an advertiser to buy branded coverage and be visible to the audience on a particular website. Therefore, all pricing selections need to be critically assessed before marketing campaign is launched or if you decide that you want to sell ads in your website or blog.

Affiliate Marketing:

Affiliate marketing is revenue sharing that occurs between online advertisers and buyers or online publishers and sellers. Affiliate marketing is results oriented meaning that the only the advertisers pays if the publishers the website owners who have add space to sell deliver actions. Payment is based on performance basis, typically in the form of sales, leads, downloads or registrations. For some businesses affiliate marketing can really perform well. With affiliate marketing advertisers become affiliates by allowing other websites are advertising networks to promote an offer. Advertisers wanting to get into affiliate marketing must have a sound way of tracking the actions to make sure that they want to pay partners correctly to make sure if the partners are tracking the actions that they are tendering exact deed counts for compensation and to track the quality of the actions. Most affiliates use third-party affiliate management software to track actions of affiliate. You can promote your products or services by having an affiliate programming or you can also explore monetizing your website or blog with affiliate ads. If you do put ads in your website to make money you do need to disclose this in your online privacy policy.

Social Media Advertisings:

Social media advertising is a form of online advertising that involves buying ads on social media sources. Social media ads are much targeted promotional options. When you create your Facebook profile you include your city, age, interests & more. Advertisers can target their ads specifically to target people based on the custom targeting criteria. Visit Facebook.com/advertising to create an Ad;

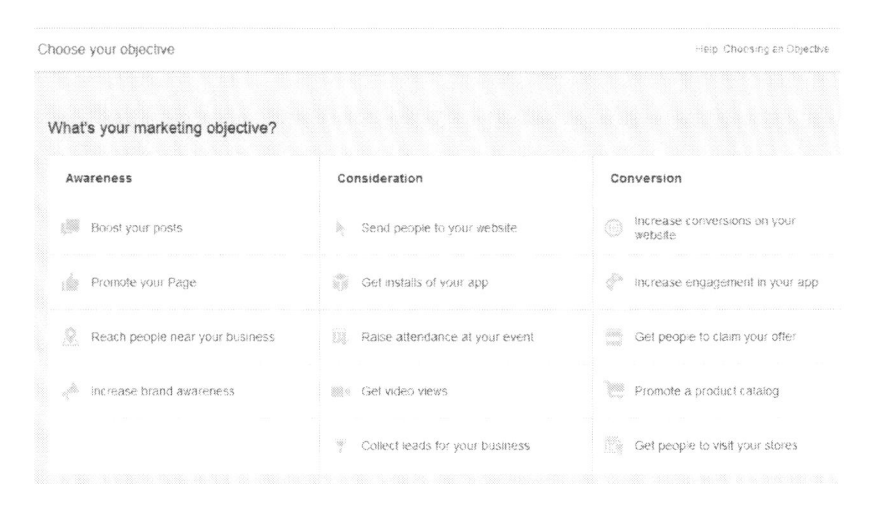

Awareness	Consideration	Conversion
Boost your posts	Send people to your website	Increase conversions on your website
Promote your Page	Get installs of your app	Increase engagement in your app
Reach people near your business	Raise attendance at your event	Get people to claim your offer
Increase brand awareness	Get video views	Promote a product catalog
	Collect leads for your business	Get people to visit your stores

You can see how the ads solutions work without placing in a credit card, so I persuade you to go there and give it a spin. Social media advertising can be tested in within industry and work-related social networking sites catering to professionals, like LinkedIn, like Facebook. With linkedIn you can call their Ads area to look how you can target by geography also get more professionally focused advertisement wise targeting like company, job titles and even age. You may be surprised when you see how it targets your ads. When the masses are using social media every day; indeed many times a day there is an opportunity to reach people but remember that your Ads have to make an impression against the sea of noise that is already happening there.

Email Advertizing:

Email marketing and email advertising are not the same things. Email marketing means sending messages to permission based catalog typically constituted by getting sign-ups of your site. Email advertising involves reaching a prospective customer in their email inbox through somebody else's list. You can buy ads, email list to reach people either in the form of having your message and or having the ad that is a part of the email newsletter. Before you buy email advertising list, make sure that the list is a quality list; meaning that people have opting into it, that the names were legally acquired and that you understand the payment terms and a help to talk to references before you buy email advertising. Online advertising is simply one tool in the online marketing sandbox. There are multiple variables online advertising presents and you have an online advertising management plan as need to be created and tested, measured, managed and optimized. There is a well-known quote *"half the money I spend on advertising is wasted; the trouble is I don't know which half"*. The man behind this message is **John Nelson Wanamaker** the man who opens the first department store in 1875. One of the largest distinctions of online advertising is its measurement power. So there is no excuse for spending money on any form of online advertising and not knowing what works and what doesn't. Web analytics can help you measure online advertising success.

CHAPTER: 4
SOCIAL MEDIA MARKETING: IN BROAD

Social media marketing with Facebook and twitter is a vital way of advertizing in social media perspective and how twitter and Facebook function jointly. We will take a quick look at both platforms what makes them unique and take a closer look at their key features and also point out methods for building quality content and way to make sure that your brand is healthy and received by your target audience.

What is Social Media?

Historically online advertising was a quite one sided move toward. Businesses pressed ideas out and consumers passively received them. However, the landscape has shifted and the internet has become extremely interactive. Social media has created a new style of communication and are now billions of conversations happening online. People are discussing popular news articles; sharing photos; their pets and even engaging with brands. These are natural to the consumer which is just part of how the web operates. All of these conversations present excelent opportunities for marketers. We can join in on a conversation to drive brand awareness or to create his/her own conversations and empower our customers to do the marketing for us.

Social media marketing is all about generating interactive moments with our customers to achieve a goal we define which is most often to gain traffic to our website or attention on our brand. But unlike other forms of marketing, social media taps into the idea of using your regulars as an advertising vessel. The main benefits of Social Media marketing are

[**Social Media marketing:**
- Create Interactive Moments with Customers
- Achieve defined goals
- Drive traffic to sites
- Get attention for brand
- Get Customers to spread the word]

The content that you share will hopefully be liked, re-twitted, and shared again, blogged. This vital effect is what makes social media promotion so effectual. An easy 'like' on a post could expose that content to hundreds of potential customers, you normally wouldn't have access. Because social media is so personal, when friends share content it comes with another layer of credibility. Right social media has the potential to transform the business. However, it will require a good strategy, some creativity and little bit of luck. Done wrong; social media might bring unwanted attention which may harm your business or your brand image. We were going to focus mainly on the organic aspects of social media marketing, more purposely the unpaid and natural approach to distributing content. For many brands, social media must have constituent of your digital marketing strategy. Your social media might feature major networks or it could be as simple as a blog customer forum, or a small nice book marking site. In this book, however all be focusing on marketing with the Facebook and twitter. Now these two networks are not the same. Each one has unique and own best practices style and audience.

Value of Social Media:

At its core, social media marketing has the ability to bring a new kind of exposure to your business by providing social media networks; such as Facebook and Twitter. You'll find opportunities to capture new customers as well as get your current customers engaged. But there is more value in social media than just brand recognition and site traffic. Let's discover some of the extra value ads, within social media; first of all social media marketing creates the opportunity to hear from your customers. Often, they will share things directly with your social channels or ask questions that might help you to identify the good or bad in your business. But beyond their direct interactions, you'll get a sense of what's important to your audience by looking at what they share and how frequently with an active viewers. You may ask for feedback or test thoughts before crafting larger marketing initiatives. Secondly, you'll establish credibility. Today's consumers are spending more time researching brands and products before spending money. With an active social media presence, you'll allow your customers to indirectly advocate for you. It will boost your overall credibility if they leaving a positive comment, sharing a review or interacting with your content. Thirdly, you'll develop a community and community is an important goal for driving awareness to your brand.

[**The value of social media marketing:**
- Hear from your customer
    Identify the good or bad
    See what they share or don't share
- Establish Credibility

Customers become your advocate
Receive positive feedback and reviews]

As customers become advocated, they turned social media to shower you with praise. It's this community that will ignite your word-of-mouth marketing and help you reach untapped territory. Friends to friends for recommendations and social media allow you to activate those opportunities and expose your brand to a new audience. Now, these are just a few examples on the value of social media. Take the time to look at your own objectives and determine what would be the biggest value for you as each value can have a different motivation. You might want to build a community simply to retain your existing customer base, whereas another business might build a community for the sole purpose of getting content to go viral.

Facebook vs Twiter:

While Facebook and Twitter share certain similarities; in both social networks you can post and consume information. There are however actually two very different platforms. twitter tends to be a public and real time feed of short paths where as Facebook is more private network used to list information and thoughts with friends & family. Now twitter has around 20% of the internet population using it and its most popular with the 18 through 29 group of crowds. It slightly biased towards women but not by much. Twitter is good for short and rapid communication and tends to be a top choice for consumers looking to get support to a brands. Twitter also has impressive mobile saturation. Around 30% of Twitter users are checking their feeds from a mobile device. In Facebook post, the highest percentage of users who graduated from college still find a strong middle class represented. A brand calls to those ages 24 to 50, there's an opportunity here. Now, younger users are shifting away from Facebook and joining to instrgam etc.

to communicate digitally. As for the gender ratio, it's fairly well split between male and female users. You can use both networks simultaneously but understanding these differences between the two will help you to determine the right strategy. So, when we think about strategy consider that twitter content has a short life span and 90% of all engagement on the tweet happens within the first hour and that number might shift if you do get tweet by a significant brand or a person. On the other hand facebook post can live on for several days. Facebook delivers content when it thinks it's most relevant to a particular user. Think of Facebook, as an ongoing conversation and twitter as a real-time instantaneous one. As you explore when and how frequently they post content, you'll find that both networks have different optimal posting times. These times will be dependent on your audience, your geographic location and the category of business you operate within. If you're just starting out, we recommend exploring both networks. Twitter is a great place for handling customer service and providing short updates as they relate to your brand. Facebook is an excellent area to shirt in-depth content and create conversations around particular topics.

Basic Necessities of Social Media:

The first thing you want for social media marketing is to make sure you're set up to collect data. Data is necessary to making decision on your social media efforts. At a basic level you should have Google analytics must be set up & running on website. It's fairly easy to get established with Google analytics but if you'd like to dig deeper check on Google analytics. Here if you like to drive traffic to your site from social posts, we also recommend creating custom links and you can track the success of each of those efforts. A great tool for this is bitly and you can find that at https://bitly.com/; simply put your URL and it will create a nice shortened version and then you can check how many clicks it received from your bit.ly dashboard. Next consider how much time you or your team to spend on social media. Plan at least an hour a day. You have got to remember that you need to write copy, make designs and find images to support your message and evaluate your results so that you can improve strategy. Think about your own experiences with brands on social media. Have you ever visited a twitter profile or Facebook page of a brand and felt idle and outdated. What perception did you have in that situation? It's never a good experience for a customer to encounter the miscellany of a failed social media plan. Next is about, what resources you have available. Are you doing this self? Can you educate an important person on your group to help you? Will you hire a freelancer once? You might decide it's worth it to pull out more helped and finally pencil out your budget. What are you planning to spend even that were not covering any paid advertising. You'll still need to make sure the time you or your team will be in spending market. Your hourly rate and include that as part of your spend time is money which means social media is actually free with your foundation set up.

Framework of Twitter:

Over 240 million people worldwide on twitter every day to talk about things that interest them, interacting with a trending topic such as the launch of a new Phone, learning about world events, talking about their day-to-day life or interacting with brands like yours. Being businessmen, Twitter is about creating and capturing these conversations. You might leverage Twitter to share details about products, behind-the-scenes like process or helpful tips that in turn boost your attention. It might even convey your brand's personality by sharing other news from your industry or adding opinion to an existing topic. As a business, the goal is to obtain followers by adding value to the Twitter network. By building followers, you can increase existing customer relationships and develop a new leads while building an existence. A major brand has an existence on Twitter; each with unique goal. But the core & the biggest benefit of being on twitter is having another channel to educate and engage with current and potential customers. Before you drive into starting or expanding your Twitter presence, it's important to note that twitter is a very well-timed network. It requires a compliance to consign to frequent posts. Otherwise, your brand runs the risk of looking decayed onTwitter. They love to give a shout out for a job well done. So, the first step for any business is to determine if you're willing to commit the necessary resources to maintain your presence on Twitter. As a starting point, site interacts once or twice a day until you see what works best for your fussy business. With the right level of promise, businesses can see great results. Twitter claims that people are 72% more likely to make a potential buy from a business after they follow or interact with them on twitter. People hear for businesses on Twitter. It's a quickest way to evaluate a brand check for special offer and see what others have to say. Use of twitter for your business the right time investment mixed with a high quality strategy will likely lead your plan to go.

Brand Presence:

The way your brand is perceived on twitter is important to your success. The most important brand element of twitter is the username and this is how people will interact with your business. So, you should take time to secure an appropriate username and most of your success will really depends on this user name.

Creating a brand presence
- Username
  Make it relevant to your brand
  15 characters or less
  Avoid using underscores
  Only use numbers if relevant
  Consider keywords

For most of brands this is easy but what if that's not available or your name is too long or not descriptive enough? If you already had a twitter username that you're not completely sold on, you can even change it. Firstly, it's important to make your Twitter handle applicable to your brand; away from anything random and instead pick something specific. Avoiding using your personal name, unless you are the brand with a key focus on the business. You only have 15 characters to work with. So, keep it short and sweet. Avoid using any underscores "_".Underscores is also harder for people to remember and it's even harder to type out on a mobile keyboard because it requires an extra button presser to define it. Also, we should avoid numbers; if the names you want is taken don't just add a number to the end of it, just consider appending the acronym. State your businesses and if you're in a touch and try to consider abbreviating parts of your name. Your company slogan is another great place to look for inspiration. Really the key is to keep on brand as possible. Now, if your business name includes numbers that obviously use them; if the relevant you also consider using a relevant keyword in your username for example 500Px in photography has a definite meaning i.e. 500 pixel; you may use number in such cases. If you think your brand would benefit from discovery through twitter search keywords, it can be a huge help if they wanted to enhance brand recognition. But the word must be in your business name. You may consider finding a way to include that keyword which will help you appear the results. For anyone who is looking for conversations around a word in your neighborhood, now this may or may not impact your branding. So you will have to evaluate what makes the most sense for your business if you do need to change your username. You can do so from your account settings but be sure to send a tweet to your followers letting them know your new name. You won't lose any of those followers but they may try to continue mentioning your tweeting at you via your old twitter handle. The next step is to build a powerful profile to build the brand presence. Your profile says a lot about your business. Your name by header image and profile pictures should all work together to tell the story of your brand. Go ahead and pulled up the amazon.in twitter page and any time someone tabs on username or visits page, they see the experience that intentionally crafted for them.

On the left-hand side of the screen, you can see that amazon.in opted to use the visual logo along with a cover photo. Here in the top center of the screen that includes a handful of video thumbnails that indicate what it is. However, it's important to remember that twitter will scale the image down to very small size and you can see that here just below the word tweets right next to the username.

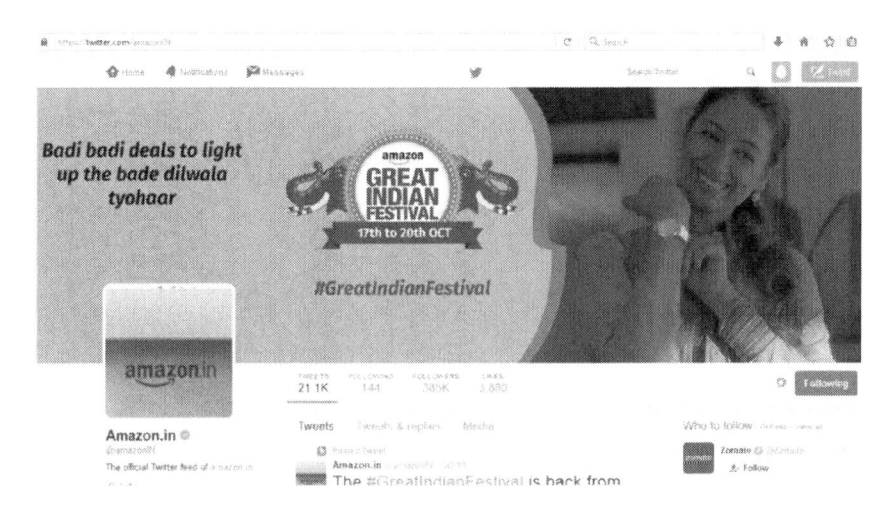

The size of logo is very small; you might want to create something unique for twitter. I recommend using an image that perfectly represents your brand; for example amazon has created a profile photo featuring an actual delivery box of amazon along with its logo. Now, if your business is your than a headshot is an ideal option and it can be looked at by clicking on someone twitter profile appear on the right-hand side of the screen and we take a look at Bill Clinton twitter profile you can see it shows users to headshot here as this profile is about him. Therefore, tweeting as a person using a headshot is a great idea.

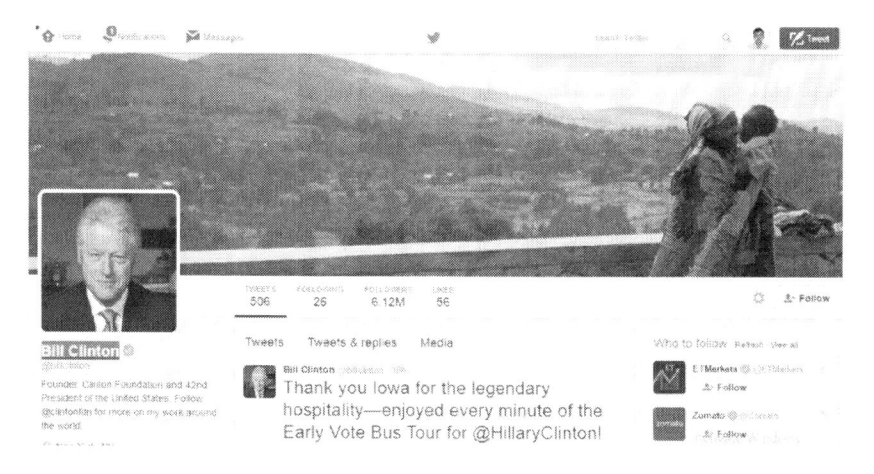

Let's go back to the amazon profile, twitter profile it is really just a landing page. Think about your own browsing habits you likely make decisions based on the look and feel of a particular page, having feels off, maybe the lack of cohesiveness or a bad color palette; you might have trouble trusting the experience. If you click on a particular product and the images are bold and radical you might either identify with the brand or be completely put off. Use your twitter profile to speak directly to the demographic you want to target. What's the most important customer for you? Build the experience for them? We can see that amazing Bill Clinton biography below the profile photo and user name but you must learn the skills you need to achieve your full potential. It short, it sweet, it's to the point and it speaks directly of the type of people likely looking. When everyone and thousands of other twitter users fighting for attention, use your profile as an opportunity to stand out invest in this experience and you have less trouble converting users to follow your brand. To drive deeper into creating this immersive experience feels free to get extra creative with your profile photo and header images which are the opportunities to showcase your brand with a large rich visual atmosphere.

Exploring the Interface:

You need to log in to set up your profile; you'll find yourself a page similar to this. So you can see here on the left-hand side it's a small miniature view of profile. I have my name, my Twitter handle, my cover photo, my profile image along with how many tweets I sent out. How to keep on followers and how my followers

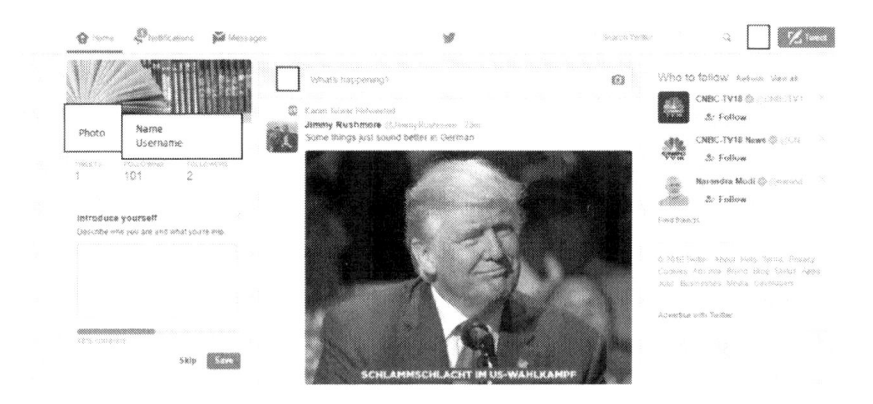

I have personally dealt. Let's start by looking at the top of the page and you find here that the home icon has a blue line under it and that indicates that we were currently on this page from here we can select notifications messages, discover or all in the right hand side, we can search twitter, interact with our profile and settings and choose to publish a tweet.

Else, we click on the notifications heading and you'll notice that this one icon above the little bell symbol. Here that you'll see the interactions with other twitter users like favorites, retwitts and who has recently followed you. Now the messages tab will show any direct messages that were sent to me from another Twitter user. On the discover tab you can explore tweets activities get recommendations on followers or even find friends. I use this section often to get a feel for what's happening; it might be a tweet or re-tweeting, the conversation worthy of a not reply or a potential influencer worth following. In the search box, we can type a phrase or word or even a user name and we can search the entire twitter environment for that particular topic. If you were to click on your profile image, you have the option to view your lists; find help, to look at the keyboard shortcuts and so on and so forth. In the upper right-hand corner if you select tweet that's where you compose new tweet or choose X in the upper right-hand corner to close.

In the center of the screen there is timeline or newsfeeds and this is going to bring all of the relevant tweets from the people that you have chosen to follow along with some Ads with twitters. Take the time to familiarize yourself with your face on twitter which is important to have a solid clutch of where to find the most pertinent information as this allows you to quickly respond to messages, craft engaging content and identify trends that might be helpful to participate.

Business Objectives:

To become successful on twitter you need to recognize your core marketing objectives. A high-level lots what you're hoping to accomplished, by understanding your objective, you will be able quickly to identify whether or not your efforts are roasted out. Now for some brands, twitter might simply be a customer support hub, a place to respond to clientele and engage with your society. The goals might be measured on the qualitative scale that is to say you'll have to decide if the quality of your engagements is worth the effort. For the brands, your focus may be the types of responses and comments your brand receives that determine how valuable the overall effort is? The last major focus for brand might be the actual sales or traffic component. You may include links to your website promotional opportunities for your products and product announcements. This objective is highly quantitative and can be measured directly through the revenue. You can have multiple objectives but the key is to identify your primary objective and build your strategy around that focus. If sales are the goal, you need to attract followers by building high quality tweets that gain threshold and include relevant calls to action to encourage the sale. But with that said you'll still want to provide customer service and generate brand recognition in the process. Take a few minutes to write out your marketing objective for twitter and decide if you be measuring the results by the quality.

Developing Communication Guidelines:

Suppose your business has an exclusive visual style. All contribute to this brand image. Your brand also has a written style; the way you write the words, you choose and the type of content you share; all make up this communication style. As you gain more and more followers, they will come to understand the style and approach. To maintain consistency and to keep a positive brand image, we suggest outlining your communication guidelines. Communication guidelines are really just a way of ensuring you not only stay consistent but will also point you in the right direction when deciding what or what not to post.

The first step all of this is to outline your voice and tone. This goes far way than just a Tweet. You should really establish this for your brand as a whole. Mailchimp has a great example of this document and you can find it http://styleguide.mailchimp.com/voice-and-tone/. If you scroll down to their voice and tone section and as you read through this you'll find that it's really descriptive process. They're talking through what their voices and giving some examples to right away. They start out by saying MailChimp's voice is human. It's familiar, friendly, and straightforward. Our priority is explaining our products and helping our users get their work done so they can get on with their lives. We want to educate people without patronizing or confusing them. As we continue we can see they have created some examples. We wouldn't say: Facebook is a great social-media website where you can create a profile and connect with friends. Facebook and MailChimp can share information, so you can add a MailChimp signup form to your own Facebook page. Instead, we'd say: Add a newsletter signup form to your Facebook profile. Here's how it works. As a scroll down further you'll notice that they create simple points of what they are and then they also have some considerations of areas where tone can be a problem. If you continue to scroll down you'll notice some key points. They talk about their brand logo and who he is and what his personality is? As you scroll through this document you can take some of these points and use them to create your own style guide. They also have a great website called http://voiceandtone.com/ and they go into more depth than you could create something very similar to this as well.

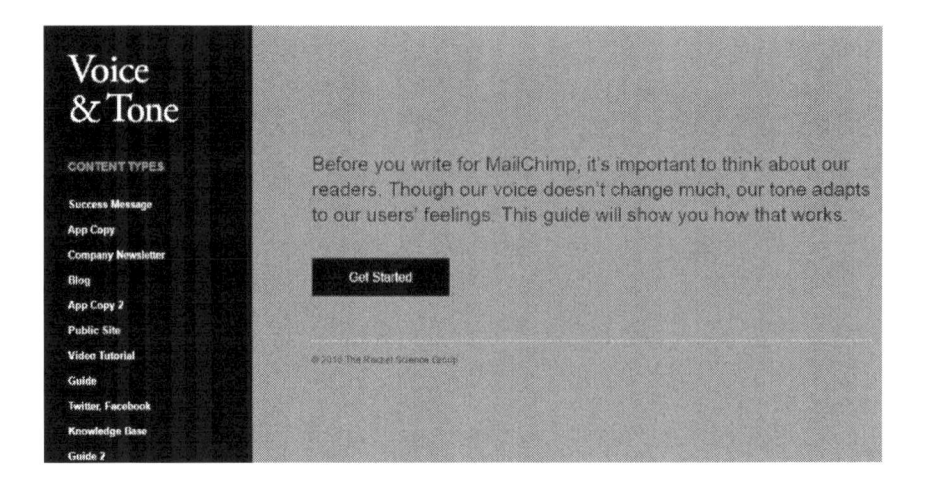

You can employ more by choosing the options on the left-hand side or just choose to get started now. This is very specific to mail chimp but there's no reason you can't adopt what they've done here for your own brand. So from here, it's time to outline your twitter communication guidelines and these are also very helpful if you work within a team. These guidelines will go beyond your voice and talk and they can be as basic as a few bullet points to as comprehensive as a response matrix dictating, the exact messages you use in various situations. Let's discuss the basic approach together. Put together a few bullet points that will help you to get started. So our main objectives in our communication:

- Be concise
- Be transparent
- Be relevant
- Be accurate

Twitters has a lot of room to describe topics. So, we want to keep things concise and highly relevant. Next, we want to be transparent and honest to say that our communication should indicate we are as a company and what's going on behind-the-scenes. Next is to be relevant; we should really only talk about topics that are relevant to our brand and are meaningful to our audience; and finally our last main objective is to be accurate but only talk about things that were knowledgeable. We really shouldn't get many conversations that we are authoritative in and have a strong background for here.

Communication Guidelines: Key Considerations
- Always add value
- Don't argue
- Admit mistakes

The first is to always add value; everything that we should be doing on Twitter. It should increase the value of our audience, so they should get something that they really want to see or read or interact with. Next is don't argue; in this really means don't get into a debate on twitter as a brand; especially over things that are important or meaningful. Also, this is always a good idea with a customer said something about your brand and it is always better to take a positive approach and argue with them positively. Third admit mistakes. If you have something wrong or happening something wrong such as you are lately reply to a particular customer question; admit it; talk about it openly. Be transparent and admit the mistake that occurred and finally always protect customers and this means going out of your way to make sure that you're protecting their privacy. You're not talking about them on twitter and you must be honest. Establish guidelines that make sense for your brand anytime; don't post something that is questionable.

Quality of Tweets:

As a business you will be bouncing tweets that maintain your community and tweets that are promotional in nature. Just as you have objective for marketing your twitter account in broad, I encourage you to have an objective for each tweet. What's the goal? A goal might be to make traffic to your website, to encourage sign-ups for an event or to earn retweets to expand the reach of your brand. To start crafting a great tweet is to first identify as goal. Next, decide what called action is required to attain the goal that might be together with a link to our website or event, along with copy that motivates click; or it might even be asking for retweet and providing an incentive for inspirational reason to do so. Once you know what your call to deed is, you can effort to weave it into a message that a follower will engage with. People more likely to share and responded tweets that inspire or entertain them, solve a problem or answer a difficult question; including a photo or video will only add to the vitality of your message. Regardless of your goal, try to keep the tweet conversational. Work towards a communication style that is genuine and approachable. If the marketing objective feels natural and unforced it will gain better traction with the community. So let's review once again what makes people share content. Because, this is really what you want to think about as you go to create these tweets. So, this is what people share if it's funny, helpful, newsworthy or inspiring.

What People Share on Twitter?
People share material that is:
- Funny
- Helpful
- Newsworthy
- Inspiring

That's really what you want to focus on. Take those into account when you craft a tweet and then take the goal of the tweet, the intended action and think of the language that needs to surround it. The surrounding language or the inclusion of a video or an image is what's going to cause your followers to interact with it. Now a well-crafted tweet is only as good as the time is delivered. So pay attention to timely delivery to take advantage of key trends existing conversations or the time your followers are most likely to be checking their feet.

Tweet Frequency:

Engaging with your audience you need to maintain a delicate balance in twitter. Tweet too much and you might lose followers; tweet inadequate and you will have fair-minded viewers. The amount of times you post to twitter each day is called your frequency. Some brands tweet each hour; whereas others can get away with a handful of tweets each week. Twitter is a real time framework, you post frequency will be far greater than that of your efforts on Facebook. The best chance of gaining interaction is by landing on the feet of your users when they are most active. Because, twitter is consequently active, your follower's feeds are altering dramatically as the day goes on. By filling up with content every second, this will award you with the opportunity to tweet frequently without coming across as excessive though. If you Tweet 10 time a day, usual followers may only observe one of those tweets and that's if you're lucky. It's also challenging though because you don't want to be recurring. You can't keep saying the same thing over and over hoping the land on someone's feed because it anytime a user can click on your username and view all the tweets. So, look at the frequency at which you are posting along with the type of content but as long as you are distributing relevant topic and high quality content you will be looked by people. It is difficult to tweet too much on twitter; so start with a high frequency and then work your way towards something that is convenient which must be effective with your audience.

Using Retweets:

Re-tweets are powerful. There's an incredible advantage to receiving a ret-weet just as much as there's an advantage to re-tweeting someone else. As a business, understanding the true value of a re-tweet will help you to find a strategy to maximize their impact. Let's review a re-tweet just briefly to make sure on the same page here is on the amazon.in Twitter page.

If I scroll down to this top Tweet here, talking about how finding out, how learning a little coding can help you do a better job. You'll notice just below the image there is an image of two arrows that make almost a circle with a number 55 i.e. that is the retweet option with 55 persons are retweeted.. If I select this option the counter their 55 will turn to 56 as it would be the total amount of people that have retweeted and then I will be posting this on my Twitter feed with the indication that it's a retweet. So my followers will know that I have taken this content from amazon.in. It will say that it's from amazon.in but also show it on my feet and to show you that vultures the retweet option. It will choose retweet and a much over to my feed and we can see here that it says I have retweeted the amazon.in tweet.

> **You Retweeted**
> **Amazon.in** @amazonIN · Oct 10
> The #GreatIndianFestival is back from 17th to 20th Oct! Is tyohaar aap kisein khush karenge? amzn.to/2dFf0R6
>
> 0:23
>
> ↺ 56 ♥ 93

So, earning a retweet acts like an endorsement of sorts; someone in your network agrees with what you're saying sufficient to publish the same communication out to their viewers. So I retweeted this amazon.in content because I agree with it. So to get traction and to really go viral, you're looking for these retweets and let's be honest any self-promotional marketing is always going to appear biased. The retweet instead gets you third-party recommendations. The more retweets, the more trustworthiness and vitality a particular communication has. Secondly, your initial audiences only so large but say you have 500 followers, the contact of your tweet to an instant audience is fairly small. Now there's an opportunity to augment visibility through several mentioned methods but the real one comes from a high-value retweet. If the user comes along with an engaged audience of say 10,000 or more followers, in this case let's say that amazon.in with its 387K followers retweeted something that I tweeted. The impact will be very noticeable; you will have a huge audience receiving your tweet in their time line. I suppose another user retweets that and another and so on and so forth you'll have a fairly wide reach and a completely new audience interacting with your content. This type of marketing is unique; it becomes user driven and you can go from one view to 1 million in moments. The trick is getting it right focusing on always building great tweets and then getting excellent relationships increases the likelihood that your message gets a retweet. Relationships are really the key to a retweet. Know the right people in your space, capitalize on trends and deliver something meaningful that they want to retweet. So, as you prospect for followers entice high-value accounts with a lot of their own followers to add you. On the other side, you have the opportunity to engage with individual accounts by re-tweeting messages they have created. Not only does re-tweeting something provide additional content for your followers but it may get you noticed by the person or company you've retweeted. Choose content that is valuable for your followers and a something they likely haven't seen on twitter before. Gaining traction even for retweet depends on being unique and timely. There's no secret recipe for viral campaigns but be creative, be authentic and stay on brand to influence users to retweet.

What is Hashtags?

The hash tag is any word beginning with the pound symbol. People use hashtags to reference a specific topics and clicking on one will take you to search results for that term. You'll see here on the amazon.in Twitter page that included the word in #GreatIndianFestival with that pound symbol in front of it and that makes this a hashtag. Now hashtag way to discover new concepts, find information and enlarge the reach of your tweet. Many conversations on Twitter involve the hashtag ; especially those that are meant for a larger audience. It's a unique way of categorizing content percent. By applying a hashtag you were essentially linking your tweet to a particular term. This term might be specific to a marketing campaign, a brand, event or a location. Hashtags increase the discoverability of content on twitter. When someone come across a hashtag, they can click on it. So here I'll choose the in '#GreatIndianFestival' and what we see all the results associated with this # and you'll see that it brings in a lot of information because the # is after all Amazon Great Indian Festival sale campaign. So, it is a great way to look for other topics and see if a particular topic is trending. Let's go back to the amazon page # such as '#Sportsnut' might be a great way for a fan to give generic shadow. It's not necessarily associated to a particular event or a larger conversation whereas a specific # such as #fashion week or #sunday night NFL will drawn lots of people talking about the same topic at the same time. Hashtags are really just a unique way of exploring thoughts in potentially real-time; for example when Apple hosted their press event launching the iPhone seven and the Apple watch people from all around the world gathered to share the reactions under a common #. when there was a technical glitch people were able to view the tweets around that # to identify that the problem wasn't unique to them; it was actually widespread. As an industry you can make benefit of hashtags. You can make a decision to create conversations round # say by hosting a contest, examination a particular operation or inquiring customers to share testimonials using your brand or you can join in on an existing conversation around #. Perhaps, you'd like to add a perspective to #music Monday or provide a special offer to anyone following #coupons. When on brand conversations are happening using # is a quick and effective way to put your tweet in front of a large audience. You can even use Twitter to help identify trending content. You can explore the Discover section of the top of the page or even search for # using the search in the upper right-hand corner. There are a lot of options on how to engage with hash tags. Search out hashtags are related to your brand service or product and then use them to interact with other influencers dominating the topic. Associate your tweets with thought leaders of your topics to start building some interest in your business. Stick to one or two hash tags per tweets and avoid including hash tags of trending topics if you aren't sure what they're referencing. Many brands have been caught in embarrassing situations by commenting on seemingly innocent trends only to find out the true nature of the topic.

Rich media in tweets

Conveying your message in 140 characters to linkages so far that extra value and context your tweets consider embedding photos or video. You will see again I'm on the amazon.in Twitter page and if I scroll down you'll see the first couple tweets here not only includes some text but also have an eye-catching image and videos. Image not really helps provide some context to what we are talking about. As you can imagine in a busy feed as users scrolling through, this image is going to pop out significantly just as a text tweet; and this is very true to the social landscape which has shifted over the years. Text updates were once the norm but now rich media is prevalent and this doesn't come as much a surprise. According to a study performed by Buddy media, tweets with images drive almost double the engagement. So, when selecting a photo or video it is important however to consider the relevancy of what you are posting. You want the media to draw attention to the post you published and that media should really reinforce the message. It can be enticing to employ an image with a lot of text overlaid on top, sort of as a way of gaining extra than 140 characters. But I suggest you stay away from that temptation. The law of twitter and why it works is because everything is so concise. The audience on twitter isn't looking for a lofty statement but that can be consumed at instant. Twitter makes it very straightforward to share images; again on using the desktop version but it's very similar on mobile. Choose the composer tweet option in the upper right-hand corner and then you can simple choose the add photo option to include a picture; from there you can follow the prompts to select the image you'd like to upload. Now, twitter has added support for multiple images in a single tweet and that is cool because the end result is sort of a miniature gallery. You might use this feature if you're posting photos of a new product, the recent event or a behind-the-scenes tour.

Now just because twitter allows for images, doesn't mean you have to or necessarily should always include the maximum. Remember the core theme of twitter is to be relevant. So if it feels like it's too much. But one thing I should point out is in addition to embedding the photo directly in the tweet, if you're looking to integrate a video; it's just a straightforward. You want to host your video on a major hosting site such as YouTube or video and from there you'll grab the link and paste it directly into your Tweet. Experiment with rich media in your tweets; a simple photo can go a long way in increasing the engagement of your post.

Focus on followers:

In order to achieve your objective on Twitter, you will require attracting more followers. More followers, the more exposure you're messaging will have. A follower is somebody who has selected to take delivery of your update in their timeline and this is the main focus of businesses on Twitter. Receiving followers is alike to receiving likes on Facebook. The difference here is that 100% of your tweets will be brought to the timeline of your group in sequential order and you can see how many followers you have your twitter profile. When you are just opening out, it is going to take some time before you generate momentum. The first hundred or consequently followers will be very demanding. But, if you continue to distribute meaningful and interesting content that number will rise. The first hundred followers can be said as your seed followers. They're likely going to be intentionally sought after. They will help to re-amplify your message to their audience and help you to find new followers. So, to find your seed followers first turn on your existing network. If you have email list of customers, a close group of work colleagues, influence the context you already have and share twitter handle with them. It's not a big commitment to follow someone on twitter. You shouldn't seed too much resistance in your task. With your initial audience in place it's time to grow and attract new followers and here's five guidelines to help you on your way; first tweet often and this means tweeting frequently every day as much relevant and exciting content as you have. You really can't over tweet as you're starting out, so feel free to try new things and experiment with lots of tweets and on that notion it's important to tweet interesting things. Your audience special your new audience has a lot going on in their feed. They only go to be interested and excited about things that are new, novel and relevant. Think back earlier when we're talking about those things that make a great tweet; third, join conversations and retweet content. Get active on twitter as you explore twitter as you have your feed reply to people, retweet content, response, great conversations and follow those hashtags; really immerse yourself in what's happening on twitter and as you do so, people come and visit your profile see what you're about and hopefully follow you. Fourth, share your profile on other mediums and this means putting your twitter handle on your website, your business cards, your Facebook page, maybe at the bottom of the YouTube video if you're doing any online video marketing. Use your twitter handle whatever you can to drive attention and awareness. Following only the relevant users and people that are going to be in your space because the ideas that you can retweet their content. You can see what's happening in your niche and you can share that and redistribute that to your audience. Keep tweeting as if you have 10,000 followers and if your messaging is unique and you target the correct audience should see some impressive gains over time.

Choosing Followers:

Once you have a rock and solid profile, it's tempting to start tweeting right away. But before you drive and it's a good thought to discover what other businesses akin to yours are doing on Twitter. Take a minute to catalog what they're doing well? What they might have done wrong and the level of responsiveness from the audience. Next, you may want to follow up core group of users. As a business who you follow is just as much a part of your brand as was you tweet. People look at who you're following and make judgments based on what they find. When you follow someone you're essentially endorsing them. With a personal twitter profile were often a lot less strict with who we follow. We may track a politically emotional outline as we appreciate the perspective and we may also follow things that we do not necessarily concur with but find value in staying connected to. As a business, it's better to put things into perspective of your audience. You might not want your business to be aligned with a political agenda. With that said, it's still important to follow people on Twitter. For one, it's important to participate in the ecosystem. Twitter is about listening as much that is about sharing. So, you want to identify things to listen to you. So, when you go to follow others think, like your business and make smart choices. Now another important factor is the quantity of people you follow. Twitter is a flexible environment; you don't need to and you probably shouldn't follow everyone back who follows you. It's tempting but it's not necessary. As a rule of thumb you typically want to have more followers than those are following. This adds to the perception of credibility and prevents your brand from looking spamming. But do what's right for your business to start following someone you can explore the Discover tab, recommendations, conduct a search at the top of the page or directly visit a twitter handle that you've heard about. Once you followed a brand their tweets will appear in your timeline and you receive timely updates; so start by identifying 10 to 15 accounts for your business to follow on twitter and then review and interact with their tweets become an active member of the twitter community.

Finding Relevant Topics and Conversations:

There's a few great ways that you can identify potential clients on twitter or even find relevant conversations. You can use search, advanced search and even explore the followers of any influencers. Now, the primary goal of search is to recognize discussion people have. People converse about all sorts of things on twitter. They discuss sports, major life events, news, restaurant and products they use. Hundreds of millions of tweets flying around twitter every day. The probability someone is having a discussion that you can add value it is really high. Have you ever been in a coffee shop and you overheard a conversation you could add value to it. Some of us jump right and will hand our business card and pitch our product; others of us aren't as comfortable with that strategy and we miss out. Twitter is like a colossal coffee shop where only you can look for the exact conversations you want to jump into and because twitter is all about having your message seen it's appropriate to send and reply to retweet or a mention when you discover a hidden gem. To be successful at search, start by making a list of keywords related to your business or products and even your competitors; then imagine yourself in a coffee shop or a tradeshow or anywhere that you are likely to find leads. Make another list of the phrases or keywords that would indicate to you; a better opportunity for you to make a sale ; maybe it's people talking about a specific issue or a problem they're having; maybe you sell digital cameras and you search for issues around. Once you've got that list you can use the search feature here in the top right corner of twitter and enter those terms. If I find a conversation that looks right; maybe someone talking about that broken camera, I could engage in them in a few ways. First, emerges retweet them if it's in line with my brand; they will receive notification and they might click on my handle to see what I'm about. Secondly, I may just apply to them; I might ask them if they've seen our business or need help with their particular problem. Authentic conversations will come across as less sales oriented and people respected. Lastly, I might mention them in the tweet; it depends on the context of what they're saying. To really unlock the power house of search, I suggest watching up and running was twitter or twitter for business. The last great way to identify leads is to look at influencers in your niche. So I could take a look at a list of followers from amazon.in for example. If I click on the following option here on the amazon.in Twitter page, I can see all of the accounts that amazon is following. I might look for a few accounts that have a lot of followers or are in the same niche as me; then I'll tweet something to them; perhaps the retweet it to their audience. Explore the various options available to you and decide which works best for finding those topics and conversations that you need to join.

Tools for Twitter

There are hundreds if not thousands of tools available online to help you to manage twitter marketing. If you're looking to go beyond the standard interface, all give you a quick look at four of favorite twitter tools. These tools might not be the best fit for your objective. I am hoping to give you a starting point and help you see what options are available in the marketplace. First tool is tweetdeck and you will find this at tweetdeck.com. Now when you visit that URL it's going to redirect you to this page here

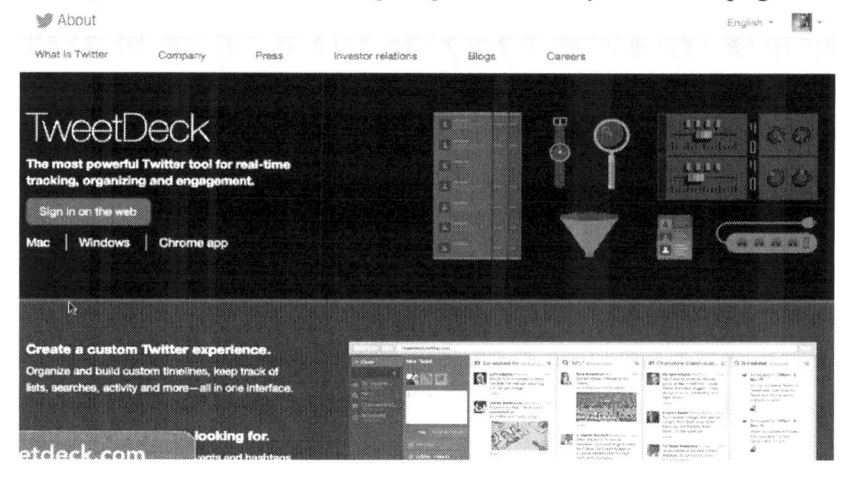

and tweetdeck is a native twitter tool. It's free and it really provides you with a source of power of options. It is a way to totally modify your Twitter experience. You can modify your views so you can have lists of search queries; say for example you want to monitor for mentions of particular topic. You can also manage multiple accounts which are great if you're keeping track of more than one brand. You can see a little bit of what TweetDeck looks like above.

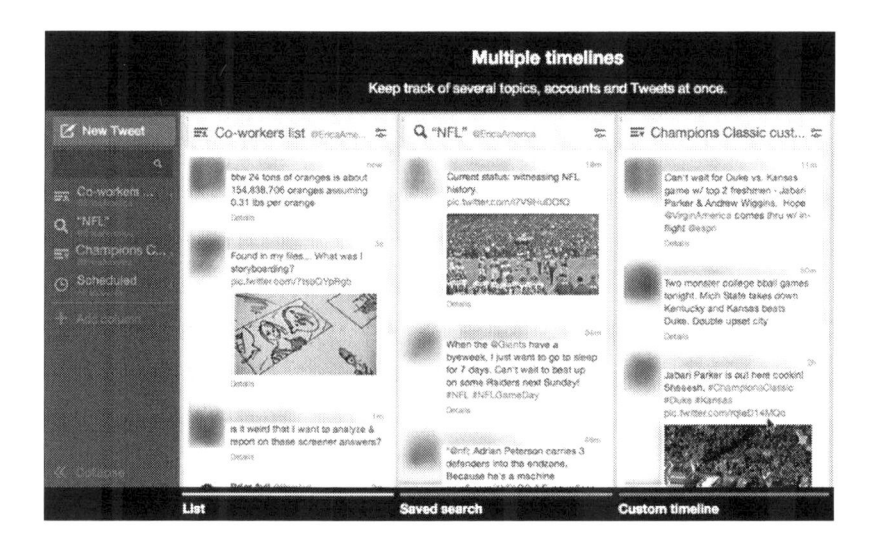

Again it's great, you can create lists, save your searches, great custom timelines and look at all of your tweets. The next tool is HootSuite and HootSuite is very similar to TweetDeck except for the fact that allows you to connect across all of your social media profiles using twitter, Facebook and Google plus. You can manage it all from one place.

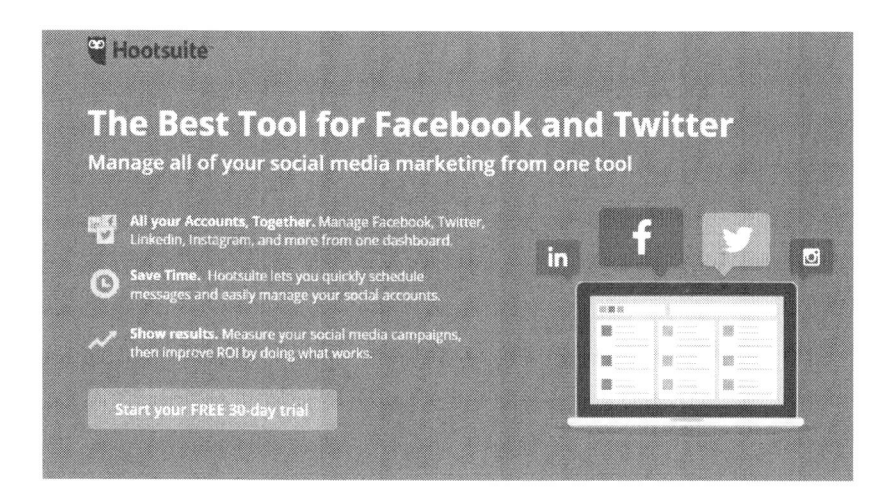

This makes content distribution really easy now; one thing I will point out is that hootsuite cost money and all clicks on the plans option; you can see what plan options are available. Do you have a free account but the features are fairly limited; in the next account starts at $9.99 amount. So keep that in consideration as you explore these tools. The third tool want to show you is called buffer and you'll find that at bufferapp.com. Buffers really cool; especially if you're trying to manage a very active Twitter feed. With buffer, you can collect content from around the web and put it all in a queue. Buffer will then automatically distribute content from your cue to your twitter feed at the frequency and timing what you dictate. Also really like that buffer has an extension you can add to your browser and this way you can quickly post relevant articles and information into your queue. Buffer is free with limited features or you can check out the awesome plan which will choose the bottom of the page and you can look at the costs associated there.

	Individual	Awesome	Small	Medium	Large
Monthly price	Free	$10	$99	$199	$399
Social Accounts	1 per platform	10	25	50	150
Additional Team Members	0	0	5	10	25
Scheduled posts per profile	10	100	2000	2000	2000

The next company I want to talk about is ifttt and you find that ifttt.com. It stands for if this than that and it's a rules-based trigger system.

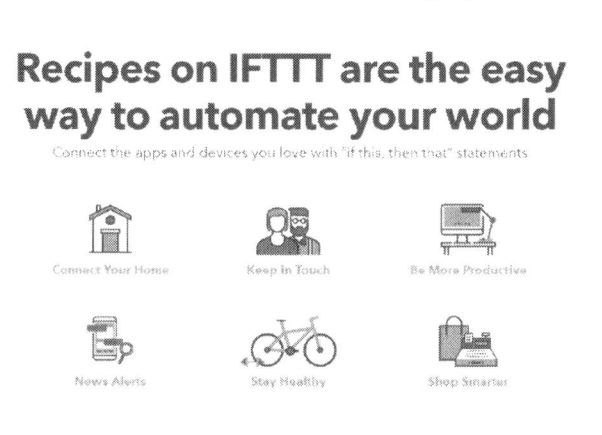

Recipes on IFTTT are the easy way to automate your world

Connect the apps and devices you love with "if this, then that" statements

So, you would set a rule such as if someone mentions my username then send me an email; I'm going to choose learn more here in the top right corner and show you what this calls for recipe and that's the if this and that this is the trigger then that in the that is the action and if you scroll down you'll see that they have all of these ingredients and recipes, away a sort of customize and create all of these various triggers and actions. You can also manage multiple accounts by setting it to automatically tweet everything you post on Facebook or your twitter account.

Customer Service Contemplation:

For many brands, twitter is primarily a customer service platform. In fact studies have shown that around 40% of consumers anticipate a reply on twitter within one hour when the connected to brand. That is a hard benchmark to strike; particularly if you're frustrating to administer all yourself. But, the truth is by exceeding customer expectations with customer service, you may really augment your sales; Twitter is public; so all of your customer service interactions are visible to others. It is really creates a unique style of transparency and it can also instill confidence among possible buyers. As they discover your twitter feed; also see how quickly you interact with problems or issues or just generic questions they will have a higher level of confidence in purchasing from you in the future. Now, what is great is that smartphones are so prevalent in today's technology landscape that it's easy to keep twitter in your pocket. So, you're managing your social feeds by yourself you can opt to receive push notifications for mentions that your brand receives on twitter and this can really help you stay in the loop and achieve that one hour response goal. As you think about how you handle customer service on twitter, take a look at a few brands that are doing an exceptional job. You can explore their Twitter feeds and little from their efforts. The first one I want to show you is McDonald's U.S. Customer Service posts and their Twitter handle is at McD Customer Service. They set up a separate Twitter account just to handle customer service and you'll notice the bio says they are here to provide McDonald's U.S. Customer Service. Here to pay attention, assist or respond any questions you have 7 days a week 7:00am to 7:00pm CST.

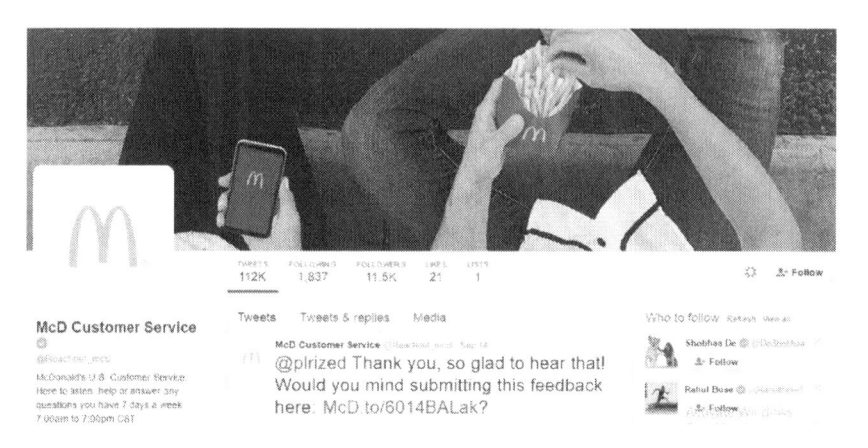

If you go through you can read through the feed and look at people's questions and how quickly and how friendly they responses are. Next is Nike support and just like McDonald, they too created a separate Twitter account. Now this doesn't mean you have to create a separate Twitter account for support. If you're a small business having the same account will likely be just fine but if you do have thousands and thousands of followers you might explore the opportunity to create a second support channel. Here at Nike lays out that there are available seven days a week and they also indicate what languages supported and again this is in their bio on the left-hand side. It is a great idea to indicate if you're only available during a certain timeline; let's say during business hours. This way people can understand when they should expect a response from you. Another great account to look at is asktarget. This is in the target general twitter account ; this is again specific to support but if you look through here you can see how quickly respond and the tone and the voice that they're using and doing so. You'll find that customers will expect to be able to reach on twitter remember twitter is all about conversations and the two-way dynamic so think about how you'll integrate customer service into your twitter workflow.

The Debate of buying followers:

There is an award for having a lot of followers on twitter. Besides the tremendous brand benefit, there is a credibility aspect that comes along with having a high quantity of followers. Since of this, many of companies have popped up that will sell you twitter followers. Companies like devumi.com, coincrack.com where you can buy followers as low as a dollar by a tone of twitter follower's even Facebook likes, histogram followers and sites are widespread. Here is another one that I pulled up buycheapfollowersfast.com.

Buy Twitter Followers Cheap, Quickly And Easily

100 Followers	200 Followers	300 Followers	500 Followers
$1 ONLY	$2 ONLY	$3 ONLY	$5 ONLY

You can get packages of 100 followers for $1; 500 followers for $5. These sites are everywhere and I'm sure you've come across and if you've done any research on this topic. But the truth is buying followers from services like this is a terrible idea. These are not real people that are either fake accounts or people who were tricked into subsequent your account. This really overcomes the idea of your marketing efforts. These accounts are not of people that are going to spread your message engage with your content or do business with you. Sure you can get the added benefit of looking popular and the business scenarios where I can work in your favor. But this effort really violates the terms and conditions on twitter and they've been cracking down and removing fake followers; fake followers don't help your credibility; they don't help your business and when they disappear; it will just be a waste of money. For twitter, you can use a free tool http://fakers.statuspeople.com/ , to identify what percentages of followers on account are genuine, inactive or fake. Now this tool probably is in 100% accurate; but it gives you a good idea. I pulled up a twitter account here called at GeekDailyDeal, which suggests that this is 63% fake followers; so you can use this tool to look at your own twitter profile to see if maybe you've got a fake followers or you can even use this tool to look your competition if you're doubtful about how many followers they have. If you're tempted to buy followers my advice don't; gain your followers organically and build a genuine user base or you can explore paid advertising methods to attract more attention your brand to using twitter adds but skip any of these sites that promise overnight followers it's never a good idea.

Twitter analytics

Twitter has its own analytics dashboard and you'll find at analytics.twitter.com. Once you're there you'll sign in with your account.

Tweet activity

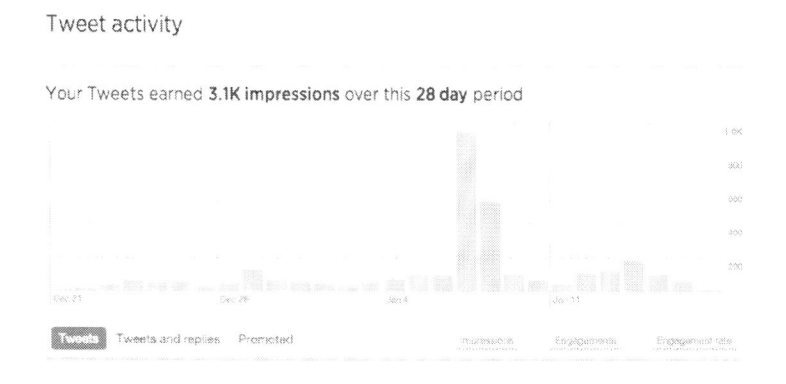

Your Tweets earned **3.1K impressions** over this **28 day** period

Along the top you'll notice that there is a headline and this headline proclaims the total impressions we've received over the last 28 days. And below that you can see each tweet along with impressions, engagements and the engagement rate. Now engagement is the total number of interactions between the tweets. This means any click on the tweet whether it's a retweet, a favorite of you, of your username etc. If we want to get the full detail we can click into a specific tweet and bring up another little dashboard where we can look breakdown of all of the information available to us. You can use these views to see overall performance and identify any outliers in your data. A strong spike might suggest some level of virility; be a retweet or a large amount of favorite the replies. To export the data you can select export data in the upper right-hand corner and what you'll get is a CSV file which can be viewed in any spreadsheet software.

CHAPTER: 5
FACEBOOK FOR BUSINESS MARKETING

Creating a Brand Presence

Now just like your twitter profile, your Facebook business page is a conservatory of your brand; how it was looked, etc. and how quickly your customers respond are all critical to your success. Now, right away here on the Facebook page for AmazonIndia, you consider they've got a visual cover photo along with the logo as the profile photo.

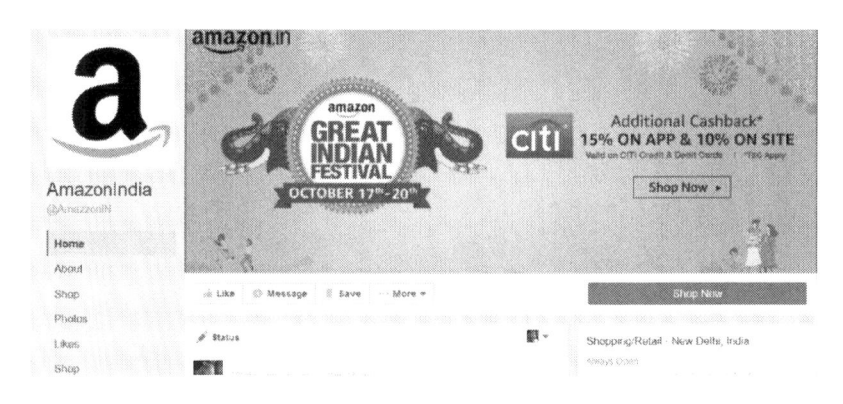

But, more than that if you scroll down on this page you'll notice where you'll see some additional information. Here AmazonIndia has opted to include a short description about what they are; along with a link to their website. You can actually add even more information if you'd like and you can learn more about that when you choose to set up your Facebook page. If I go back to the timeline you can see that a Facebook page also includes photos; so we can click in the photos to see all the photos that AmazonIndia has published and those can even be organized into albums. We can also see the likes and if we click more we can see any custom pages that Amazon has created. Now to set up a page, you'll start out by logging into your personal Facebook account and your personal account won't be visibly connected to your business page. So, it's ok to be using your personal account and from any Facebook page; you can choose the crate page option in the upper right-hand corner or visit Facebook.com/pages; where you have the option to create your own Facebook page and you'll follow the prompts and the instructions to go ahead and do so.

Be relevant; pick the right category and be sure to include a link back to your website. As you build out your page, think about your target audience you identified in your marketing strategy and then post content that will engage them. Visitors who choose to follow you might see those posts in their feet. A typical Facebook user follows many pages and has a lot of friends posting updates; so more engaging and relevant your content, the better likelihood it has of being seen. So, be sure to experiment with different kinds of posts; you can find out if your audience loves photos or if they prefer you shared useful links. I recommend that you leverage your existing marketing channels to drive awareness to your Facebook efforts. It can take time to get a meaningful audience but if you continue to deliver quality content you'll eventually find meaningful traction.

Interface of Facebook:

Facebook is fairly spontaneous and I would like to give you a quick tour of the interface for you to know what to expect. Now, I'm logged in and I'm visiting this page AmazonBest Deals which I have decided and since I am in admin of the page when I visited I get a little different view than what the public sees.

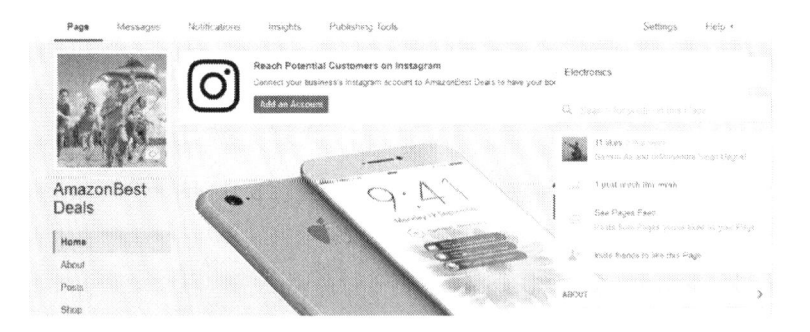

The field right away at the top of the screen, I have the page option highlighted. There's also an activity tab and the settings tab; along the right-hand side we have a build audience dropped down; which it was some paid options and free options, of inviting friends and the ability to get to the ads manager and if we need help, we can find that in the top right-hand corner. Here, on the right-hand side we have some glance information; so you can see how many page likes; we received this week and how many unread notifications and messages we have. Now, this page doesn't have any activities so that's why we're seeing little value. In he upper left-hand corner, we can change the profile picture. One thing that's great is if you choose the activity tab, you can view all of your notifications, messages and requests in one place.

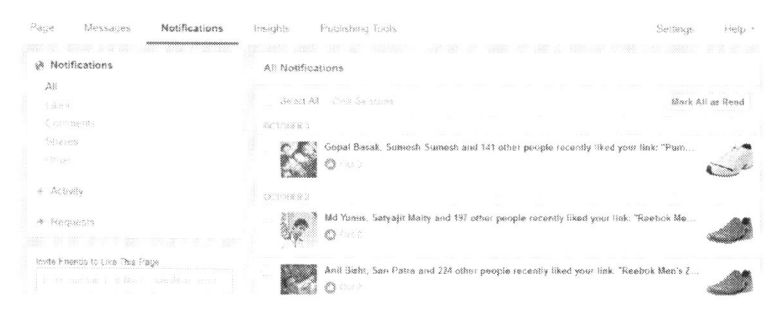

It is also a great place to see any post that you have scheduled or any drafts of content that you've created. Here in the bottom left-hand side, you can invite some friends to like this page; next is the settings tab and this is where you can configure all of the information about your page. The first thing we have is some general settings and this is your page visibility, how people can contact you, any moderation such as words that are blocked from your page and even the ability to turn on the filter. So along the left-hand side we can view various information such as apps, page roles notifications. You notice that this page info section here is the second option and if you click on it it's going to tell you that this has moved. So if you're using Facebook, you'll now have to go to the about tab and is a link here to that visit about top.

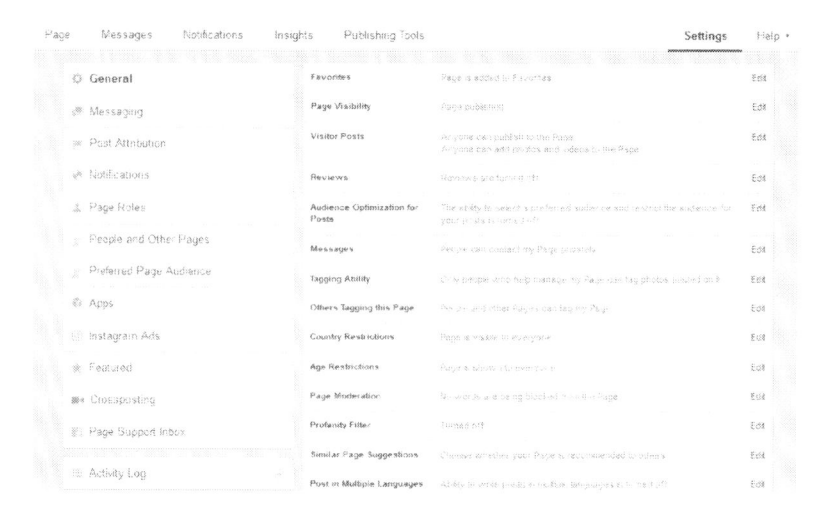

So, we go here and you can see the about tab is selected; just below the cover photo. This is where you can edit all of your page information. It is also where you can get your custom Facebook address by choosing the enter a Facebook web address option and you can follow the prompts there to create a web address for this page. Facebook does have a mobile application called Facebook pages which is a worthwhile download if you be interacting with your marketing efforts on the go.

Define Your Objective:

Just as we did with twitter, we need to describe core marketing purpose on Facebook. Facebook has a different audience and the way people interact with topic is somewhat dissimilar. With Facebook you have the opportunity to present long form content that is anything that exceeds 140 character and your twitte could be exceed 140 characters. But in Facebook posts, you have longer topic; also you will discover that Facebook doesn't insist the quantity of updates that twitter does. So, you can get away with a few of posts a day and as the lifespan of content on Facebook is lot longer than twitter's tweets; so you can think that as you describe your objectives and decide how much time and energy you put into various contented pieces. Your main goals on Facebook are likely going to be generating a friend base and this is done by receiving people to like Facebook page. So whereas on twitter you'll be gaining followers; on Facebook you beginning friends. You can then leverage this audience to accomplish your business objective and much as we saw again with twitter this might be to generate brand awareness, increase sales, drive traffic to your website and so on and so forth. Your objective will dictate the type of content you promote and with what frequency; as with most social media a main objective is to publish content those are really meets your business goals but is also unique enough to be shared and liked. These actions help promote your content to a broad audience.

Deliver High-Quality Posts:

The first step in making high quality content for Facebook is deciding on your goal. In other words what action wants a user to capture after they read your content? We may compel them to take that deed and what sustaining information can you offer to help combat any doubts. Take a minute to answer those questions since doing so will help you by a framework for building that high quality content. High quality content actually require linking with your viewers with the right message at the right time and as you go about developing your content, considers that more than a third of Facebook users are viewing from their mobile device and this means that the amount of content displayed on the screen for truncates is going to be less. You may want to try to aim for around 250 characters. Your audience might enjoy long form content or even extremely short status updates. But, if you need a place to start, try to aim for 250 characters; and that is a good starting place and it keeps your content easy and unpalatable. The type of content you decide to promote will also way into the quality of your post; consider using eye-catching images with any content you post; you can even experiment with using links or videos as both are something that Facebook supports. When you're just getting started, it's a really good idea to try all kinds of different posts to see which one gets the most attention. Visual posts tend to look better and also get a lot more shares , likes, & comments than other type of posts for most brands. You can also try post that is offers or even creating an event for a special occasion. Use the level of responsiveness on each particular piece of content to engage how well it does. This way you can compare how well photo to your audience versus say a strictly text post and experiment; try throwing in info graphics maybe behind-the-scenes photo. Change it up from time to time and see if your audience responds positively.

Facebook Post frequency:

Fewer people may be seeing your page posts because of a decline in organic reach which is the amount of content shared on Facebook grows faster than people's ability to see it. This means that your content is opposing with other stories to get placement in the users newsfeed. So with that said, it's not quantity that will resolve this problem. The main factor was Facebook is focusing on quality. Posting irregular, quality content is always going to be out the strategy of posting low-quality high-frequency content. Now another factor in reach is timing. Let's say you have often deposed to status updates per day which is a standard frequency. The time that those two posts go out; in other words at noon or 2 PM or 4 PM will greatly impact their visibility. This comes down to when your audience is online. If there on Facebook during lunch, the distribution of your content just before lunch will likely lead to a higher percentage of users seeing account. Now, just keep in mind n that Facebook determines the final relevancy. So if you're promoting say a lunch special at a restaurant and its very time sensitive. A Facebook post is probably going to miss the mark. Facebook might delay the distribution or it might even continue distributing it throughout the day; maybe even to the next day. Twitter however is fantastic and now a quick way to engage the best time to post content is by looking at your audiences activity level when their online and you can do that by clicking on the insights tab from your Facebook page and then choosing the posts option and then the when your friends are online auction which is the page that I'm on here. Keep in mind you won't have access to this data, if you have less than 30 likes on your Facebook page. If you can't find it that's likely why. We are looking at a graph of a recent one week when our users are online and you'll see here that I've got real low activity from 2 to 5 in the morning and this is going to be in your local time zone. So I'm in the Pacific time zone so this is going to be specific to me if you were in Eastern or Central and so on, the time zone would adjust to your time zone. So I can see here that the high frequency of my users are here at noon1 followed by 5 PM and this is pretty typical you'll find with most businesses noon his lunch hour for people that work 9-to-5 than 5 o'clock they're getting home or just leaving work and checking Facebook again. So, the really good times to post of a great time is seven which tends to be after dinner. I really recommend starting with one or two Facebook post today delivered during the time when your audience is most likely to be online but as with everything experiment and find out what works best for your brand.

Rich media in Posts:

On Facebook, photo posts are king and the rapid success of platform such as Instagram and pay interest which are very image heavy; only help reinforce that idea. People love looking at photos and they are a grand way to drive extra consideration to your posts. Now, remember when you select an image or photo make sure to keep it relevant to your brand for your message. I've gone ahead and pulled the Facebook page for jetairways and get a sense of what a different brand is doing.

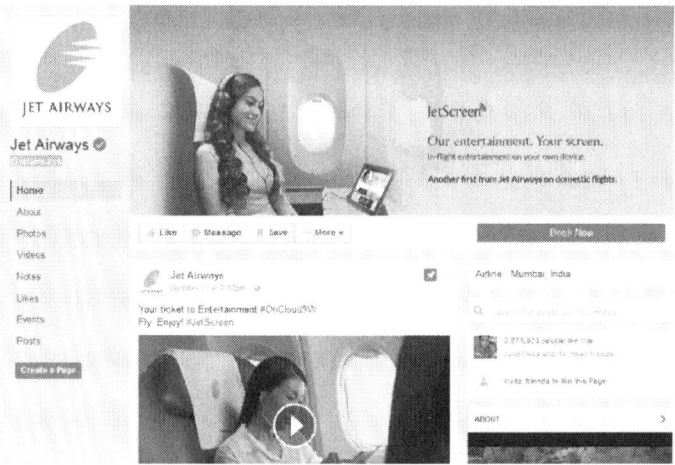

Now, scroll down the page you can see what they're using visual images along with video in all of their Facebook posts and this again helps reinforce the idea that photos are popular. If I go to the yatra.com Facebook page you'll see that they're following that same idea, big rich imagery that catches your attention and reinforces the text of the actual post.

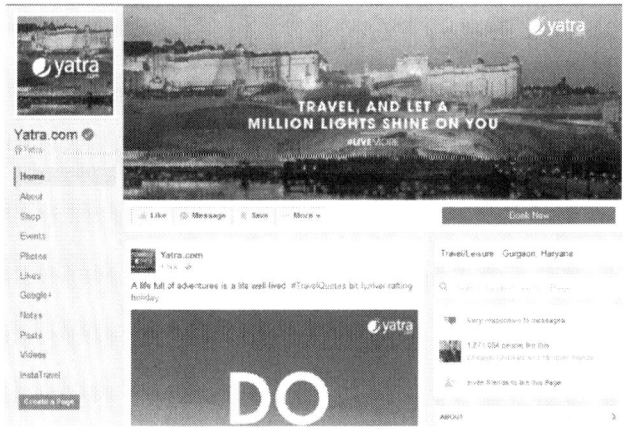

When you go to add rich media there's a couple ways that you can do it. First in your status update section you can choose the photo/video option and then simply select to upload photos or video file or you can even create a photo album which has multiple photos associated with your post.

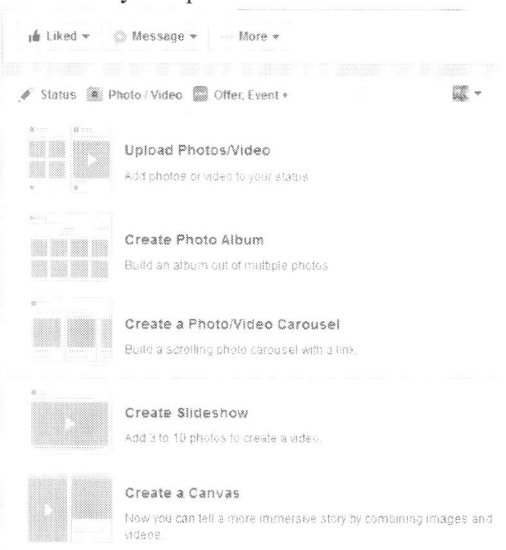

Now another with you can do this is by pasting in the URL of the content you want to share. You'll see that right away what Facebook does is it grabs the relevant image from the website and automatically positions and places it for you so. Here you can see it's grabbed the screenshot from Photos. If you wanted to change that you can choose the uploaded image option. Now, you can even go in and delete the link from the status update and write something different. Experiment with rich media in your posts because a simple photo can go a long way in increasing engagement of your content.

Growing Your Friends Count:

With your Facebook page under way, you may be looking

to gain those all important friends. As you increase your friends base, you'll be increasing your reach. The more friends you have, the more opportunities your content is seen and shared. So, Facebook friends likes to comment or share one of your posts, their network of friends and family see that backing on their individual news feed. For example let's say that you saw this post. Have you had your multi view's today either here on the business page or in my timeline and if you like it, you will choose the like option as a person what would happen is Facebook might then distribute that to my friends in their news feed. So they would log into Facebook and see that you had liked this particular post by business page and their potential been compelled to either read the content and click the link or move on to your Facebook page. Now, the truth is you would hope that this causes a user to then visit your Facebook page and like you. So, they see this content they then click on business page, they come to your Facebook page and a click like; but that's rarely the case. Friends usually don't do that; so the first thing you want to do as you begin to establish your Facebook page is grow those initial likes and then we'll talk about ways to get people to make that conversion to like your page been just a minute. So the first steps are to gain those first friends and you can do that by letting people know about your page and it's fairly straightforward. So, from your Facebook page, in the upper right-hand corner you'll choose the build audience drop-down and you'll see that you have some options; invite friends, suggest page and promote page. Now promote page will be a paid options; you have to pay for advertising to drive awareness to this page and if you're interested in that take a look at Facebook advertising fundamentals to great starting point for that. But in this case we just want to do it for free and so I can do the first option and click invite friends and what they'll do is let me type in any friends connected to personally on Facebook and I can invite them to come like the page. You might be more interested in is sending out an email to anyone in your contact list. So if you have a list of current customers say in mail chimp or just in your own email client you can take that mailing list and send everybody a notice that says they come like my Facebook page and you can do that right from the Facebook interface by choosing the suggest page option. So, I selected this with a pop-up and we can upload a contact list file we can even upload her contacts if you're using mailchimp constant contacts or even Yahoo you'll simply follow the prompts after you click upload contacts put up to 5000 emails in and send off an email.

The next big question is what motivates someone to like a Facebook page and typically it's usually an incentive. So users are highly motivated by special deals, offers, coupons so that they couldn't get outside of this Facebook page. So, look to create unique opportunities for reasons as to why fans should like your page. Now, historically you were allowed to trade content for naturally or organically and that's a good thing because you really do only want people who genuinely want to like your page interact with your content will be a much better experience. Now, a great way to get more likes on your page is to install the Facebook like button on your website or blog and you can do that by using the Facebook developer section. To get here you go to **developers.Facebook.com** and then find the sharing tab on the left and to social plug-in; alternatively you can go directly to the URL **developers.Facebook.com/docs/plug-ins/like-button** or do a Google search for Facebook like button and you'll get this option here to customize a like button.

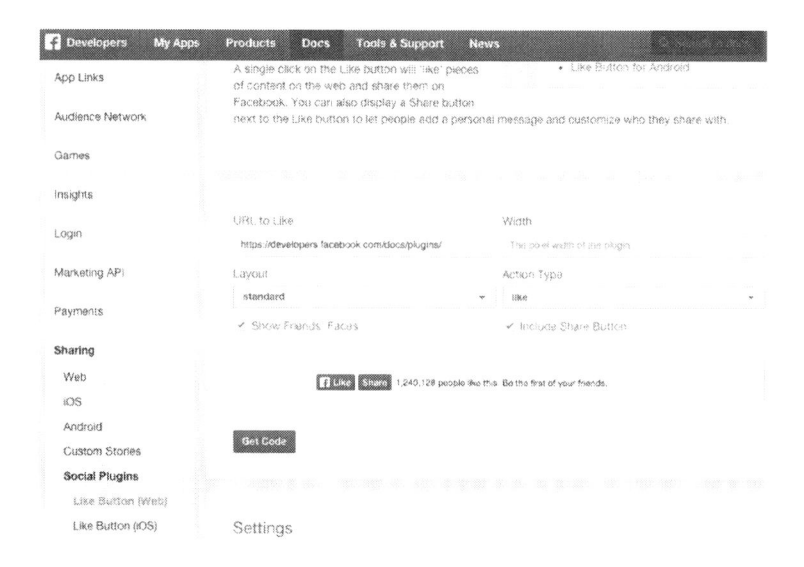

It says URL to like and they put in the developers URL to start. Which you want to do is paste in the URL of your Facebook page. Now export doesn't have their own custom URL yet but if you did have your own custom URL you could paste that there as well. What you see happens all click on the box and the preview shows you what this looks like and who else likes this page. You can modify that by unchecking the show friends faces; you can uncheck the include share button and you can also use the drop-down to change the layouts. If you wanted the box count which looks like this you can select from the layout drop-down.

Adding Page Tabs and Apps

One unique feature to Facebook is the ability to increase the capabilities of your Facebook page through the use of page taps and a Facebook page tab is essentially a link to a third-party application that integrates itself directly into your Facebook page. This is great because it allows you the opportunity to add new functionality while still staying within the Facebook environment. Now this application is actually built, maintain and running on a third-party company called woobox. But it still within Facebook and I can use my Facebook account to directly interact with this and it has a great functionality because the new way to get users to engage. So, let me show you the company behind this application is called blue box and we went ahead and visit their site woobox.com.

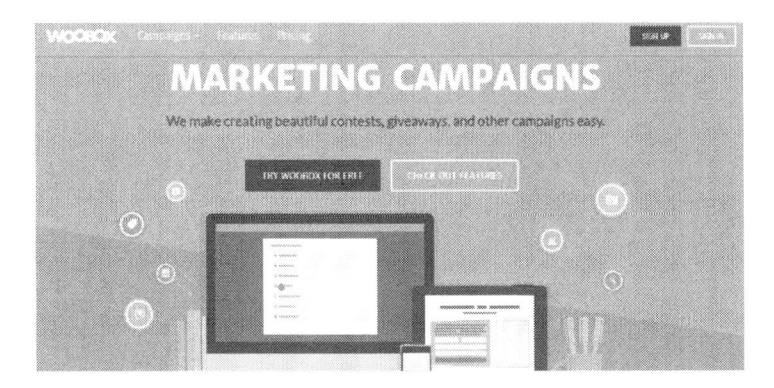

You can see here as I scroll down that the let you create all kinds of promotions: sweepstakes, photo contests, even they have tabs for twitter. There's all kinds of great options here and there's a lot you can do. So you want to check it out and explore it on your own time. Another great company to look at is shortstack.com. In the example section and all scroll down just to get a sense of some ideas beyond woobox. Here they've got some goal oriented options such as boosting engagement and they've got a great drag and click interface, making it really easy and intuitive to build these page tabs.

Third-party applications go a long way and their excellent resource to building interactive and engaging content beyond the typical Facebook.

Winning your Friends:

To build a thriving community on Facebook, it's important interact your friends. Aside from working to create high-quality content, be sure you're staying on top of your comments and feedback. Friends appreciate brands that take the time to respond and its common practice to reply to friends comment straight on your Facebook. Use that opportunity to direct them to alternative support channels such as a phone number or email address. Now, away from responding, there are other ways that you can engage your audience. You can share ideas, ask questions and ask for feedback straight from them and even create unique opportunities for participation; as for example you may decide to use a third party application to run a contest or you can even keep things simple by asking friends to upload photographs using your result for a possibility to win. Now, I pulled up to examples of Facebook content that I think is a really good job of demonstrating this idea of engagement. The first comes from LL Bean Inc;

They create a custom image of their flagship store and it's a historical photo and they go on to explain the store has been open 24 hours a day seven days a week since 1951. In the last primary times how many times the store actually closed and everyone submits their suggestion and they come back in the answer the question and it's a great way of getting people to respond and like. Growth on Facebook is hinged your ability to engage with your friends so reply interact and create unique opportunities for them to participate.

Facebook analytics:

Facebook makes it easy to review how well your pages growing and provides helpful metrics so that you can determine what types of content your audience akin to best which is called your Facebook insights and you'll arrive to it by choosing the insights option from your Facebook page and lend here on the overview tab.

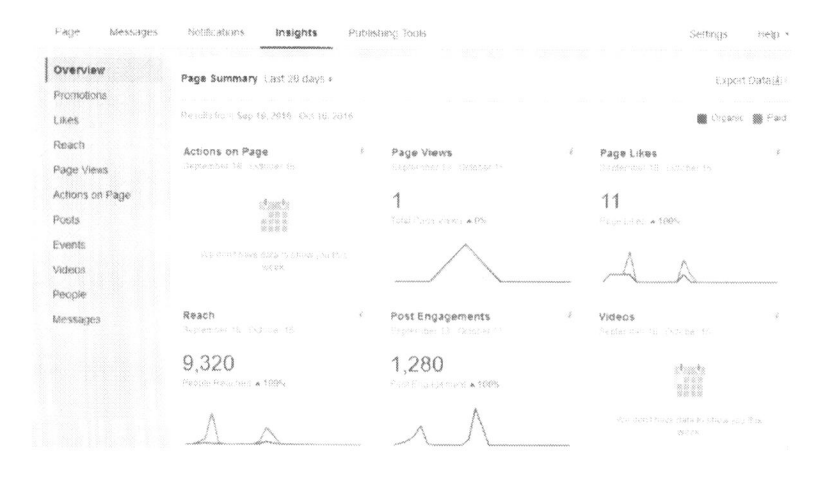

Now you can only access insights if you have more than 30 Facebook friends. At a glance we can see our page likes, post reach and engagement and here are page like show us our total page likes which is 11 and then what percentage of those are from last 28 days. Lets me know that our page is n't growing and I might want to explore some engagement opportunities. In the center is our post reach and that is to say how many individuals have received our content on their timeline. Now there's no guarantee that they've actually read it; because scrolled right way. But, we know that we landed on their timeline and in this case that 9320 people which is up significant. Next, we have our engagement and this lets us know how many people have liked, commented, shared or clicked on an actual post. This case we've had 1280 engaged people which is up 100% from last week. Now along the top here, you'll notice that we have some other options likes, reach, visits, posts and people and here we can explore the various contents. So, if I click on the likes we can get a granular view of exactly what's happening. Here at the top we were historical timeline and we can adjust the dates on the right-hand side and if I scroll down we can even see are unlikes organic likes and paid likes before running paid promotion. You'll find that these charts and graphs are all unique to each section and I encourage you to explore them in your own time and make a habit of checking in on your Facebook analytics daily because being familiar with your data will help you make key growth decisions.

CHAPTER: 6
E-MAIL MARKETING

This section of the book is designed to give you tips and advice for growing your business or organization with email marketing by showing you how to get your email marketing program off the ground and how to build your email list while comply with system and consumer favorites. Then we will discuss which types of email content and designs are most effective and tips for coming up with good content and making your content more valuable.

Email Marketing Basic:

In business, you need to communicate with lots of people to attract customers. Your business also needs to make sure that your communications for marketing carry in revenue over and above the cost of those communications. Email is a great explanation for structuring customer relatives affordably because it's a familiar communication standard and it is also cost effective. The fact that email is a cheap way to communicate is the main reason to use email. However, return of email is very high or in other words an effective email marketing strategy can create a lot of sales for comparatively little investment of time and money. In order to get the highest possible return your email marketing investments, you first need to understand where to use email in your overall marketing plans. Firstly , sending email to total strangers does not work. You're more likely to get spam complaints been interest from prospective customers unless you sent to a permission-based email list. Instead of people use email to help convert current forecast into customers and current customers into loyal customers. Using only to educate people about the features and benefits of your products or services differentiate your business from your opposition and to request for the sale. You can also use email to help increase customer loyalty and referral by sending emails that make stronger your customer relationships. Send Banking emails, holiday greetings and offer special benefit to make your customers feel like they are esteemed one. No matter what kind of business organization you have keeping your customer relationships is at the center of your policy that will put you on the road to email marketing success.

Technology for E-Mail Marketing:

You'll need at least two technologies to execute your email marketing strategy; and authoring technology to create the content of your emails in HTML and delivery technology that has the ability to deliver and track email send to a large email list. In order to do literally everything, you are required to own your own email server. I don't recommend doing completely all in house even for a bulky business with lots of technical resources; instead of using email marketing supplier or EMP to assist you to scamper your policy and EMP is a company that offers a suite of tools to help you create send and track your marketing emails. Most EMP is allowing you to create emails without the need to know any HTML programming languages and you don't need to setup and manage your own email servers and delivery gateways because EMP is send email from their servers on your behalf. The customers will never know the difference and you probably get better delivery rates too. EMP is give you tracking reports and database tools to manage your email lists and some EMP is even provide support and educational resources to help you gain expertise in marketing and the use of the EMP's tools. Enterprise-level EMP is give you access to advanced features such as point-of-sale integration, email automation, advanced segmentation and behavioral targeting. Remember that one of the most important assets of your email marketing strategy is your email database. Make sure you use a company that secures your email database properly; protect the privacy of your email list subscribers.

Can Spam Act:

There are laws against unsolicited email or spam because people hated that and the government makes rules here's what you need to know to become appreciated email sender. Let's start with the law and about to say is not legal advice in any way; it's just a summary of possible issues use a licensed attorney to make sure you follow a law when it comes to email marketing. The main law governing commercial email is known as the **Can Spam Act**. The major guidelines of Can Spam Act are: First and foremost you need a relationship of positive consent between your business and anybody to whom you send marketing email. You also need to provide an easy and at no cost way for your subscribers to option out of receiving future emails. The industry standard is one or 2 clicks to unsubscribe. Moreover make sure the information in your email is true and accurate; not allowed to figure online users misleading subject lines or send email from a false email address. Finally, make sure you include your physical business address and every email; given your emails legally compliant with keep you out of trouble with the government but your job as an email marketer isn't to make the government happy; your emails is to impress prospects and customers. Here are three tips to make sure your email marketing is well received and appreciated by your subscribers; first ask for clear authorization before distributing marketing emails. Second, ask your subscribers to share their preferences when they connect your email list and send the information only your subscribers request. Third make sure that you send emails with the suitable frequency and significance. In general, people will tolerate almost any angle frequency as long as you're in all content is valuable and relevant; for example whether it is a daily occurrence, so whether information is likely to be valued on a day frequency. If you send a daily email asking people to buy something however you'd better be pretty sure that your subscribers are interested in daily deals.

Creating Email List:

Email marketing without permission can bring disaster for your email marketing. You can't legally send email to total strangers and even if you could; it does not make any people happy by sending them emails they didn't ask for. Therefore an email list without permission is very priceless; however when an email list includes the email addresses of prospects and customers who have explicitly asked your business to send an email to stay informed, you have a very valuable asset for your marketing strategy.

The first step in the process of building a permission-based email list is deciding on a permission level. There are three basic types of permission, the lowest permission level is implied permission; for example when someone hands you a business card says let's stay in touch you could assume that means sending a few emails but be further careful with oblique authorization as people may be unpleasantly surprised if you start sending marketing emails without initial authenticating the content & the frequency of those emails. It is a good idea in the case of implied authorization to send an email authenticating your choice to add someone to your email list and include a link for opting out if your new implied subscriber doesn't want to be on your marketing email list. The second permission level is explicit permission; for example someone fills out an online form to join your email list that person is given you explicit permission to send emails as your email sign up for specifies. Explicit permission is the industry standard for email marketing and the suggested level of consent for email marketing providers. The third permission level is confirmed permission also known as double option in. Confirmed consent works like this when someone explicitly option to your email list you said email asking the new subscriber to confirm their decision to join the list. Usually this happens by clicking a link or replying to the verification email with a precise message. Confirmed permission insures that your email list subscribers are highly involved in receiving your emails and confirming permission generally improves your delivery rates too. You should avoid building your email list based on someone else's permission for example don't send marketing emails to people on email lists wanted your vendors your colleagues your partners or trade organizations. If you want to arrive at people on other email lists inquire the owner of the list to send emails to their list on your behalf and ask them to explicitly opt in to your email list. If you decide to use a list broker anyway, make sure the list broker uses completely compliant with all laws and industry best practices. Since your email list is valuable protect it like an asset. Don't share your email list with anyone and don't violate your permission standards by sending emails your subscribers didn't sign up.

Collect information:

When we come to collect emails, there are five basic ways to ask people to join your email list. The first way to collect email addresses this by providing an online sign-up form to your website. Visitors should put the sign-up form or link to the sign-up form on every page of your website; not just the homepage because you never know someone will enter your website or exit your website. The second way to collect email addresses is to collect email addresses from people in person when one calls your business on the phone asked if he or she would like to join the email list to take delivery of in order about the topic of the call. When you attend networking events such as trade shows when you meet people for appointments ask everyone to join your email list. I call it the 5 foot rule if someone is within 5 feet 2 inch of you request for his email address. Thirdly, all printed marketing materials should describe a method to connect your email list. You may provide a sign-up form by asking people to write their information openly on the form and you can use printed publicity to promote other methods of joining. The fourth way to collect email addresses is through mobile devices. You can ask people to scannable barcode.

This one actually works give it a try right now in your screen to join the email list. You can also asked people to text their email address to join and you can provide mobile sign-up forms that can be complete out on a smart phone or tablet device. You can use mobile devices for collecting addresses of persons as well by; simply hand your device to someone so he or she can fill out a form on the screen. The fifth way to collecting all addresses is through social media networks. Place sign-up links to your email sign-up form on social media websites you won and promote your email list in your social posts. Some social sites such as Facebook allow application plugins you can embed forms directly in your page. Remember that an email address is more effectual when combine it with other information; you may want to collect a first name for personalizing your emails or ZIP Code for targeting local authors. But don't ask for too much information the first time you sign up or to reduce sign ups. You can also ask for additional information once you establish a relationship of trust with the members of your email list. Collecting email addresses and other personal information isn't always easy.

Incentives for customers:

It's a common misconception that people are not willing to share their email addresses. Actually, they are like to share; you just have to converse the value of your email list effectively. The ideas exchange value for information; the more valuable your email the more people will sign up to receive that value. But there are three essential behaviors you can make the most of the value of subscribing to your email list. The first way is to make the information you set in your emails precious. For example a advisor could offer free advice via his or her email newsletter. You can also provide your subscribers instant incentive for joining email list. Immediate incentives are usually offered to subscribers in the shape of an automated email sent to the email address used for the subscription. Use your automated emails to send discount or a coupon, a precious download, access to a special video, free product or service or anything else that has instant advantage to the new subscriber. For the best result offer something related to your products or services as opposed to offering a free gift on related to your core business; that way you get a prospect who is just as interested in what your businesses is what you're giving away; for example restaurant could offer a free meal anyone who links the email list by transferring a coupon to everybody who subscribes. In addition to immediate incentives you can also present the same reimbursements in the future. The benefit of future incentives is the fact that you can send new subscribers a few emails before they receive the incentive.

Designing an Effective Marketing Email

Marketers directs to the format of an email, it implies that the layout of the content in the purpose of a particular email, work togetherness & functionally as an unit; for example a newsletter is an email format. It is important to use a diversity of email formats for two reasons; first people respond to different formats in different ways; for example many people likes to read an email that looks like a newsletter while in an email that looks like an urgent statement is more likely to get instant notice.

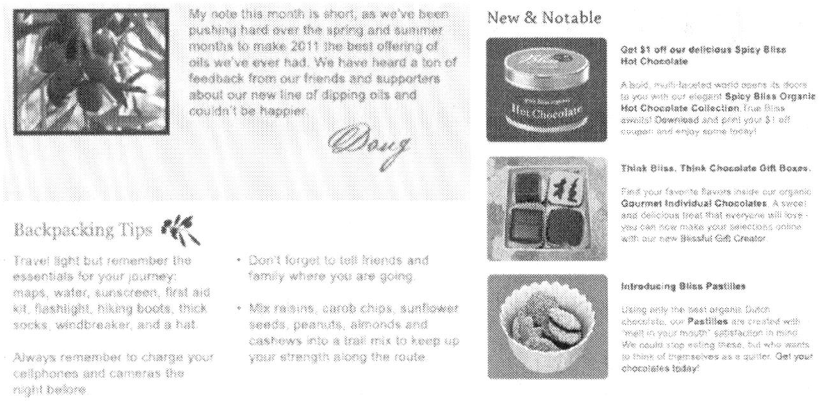

While getting immediate attention for every email might sound like a good strategy; however the reality is that urgency wears off if you use the same email formats for all your communications; second reason is to use a variety of formats. You need as many formats as you have reasons to communicate; example if you launch event, promotions, invitations, news information, greetings and appointment confirmations. You should use sufficient email formats to appropriately categorize your information into logical groupings. Email newsletters are typically listening carefully on in order rather than promotion. Newsletters can have columns to give them the form of a paper newsletter and are great for sending loosely related information in a single email. Newsletters also should have a cyclic frequency such as weekly or monthly rather than an event or date driven frequency. For best results diminish the amount of promotional content in your email newsletters. No more than 20% of your email newsletter object should surround promotions. If you need to promote more than that, use promotional email format. Promotional email must focus on a sole promotion such as a single product or group of related products such as a sale. Promotional emails are usually date driven or their triggered by specific actions such as a recent purchase, order inquiry. When using promotional emails, it's best to put some but not all of the details about the promotion in the email itself. With the rest of the details on the website, you should invite people and so you know how many people were interested in learning more about the promotion. Another type of promotion is an event invitation. Event invitations can focus on one event or a series of events. Events are highly date driven; usually require a series of emails and similar formats to get a good overall response. Make sure you plan out your event invitations on a calendar to avoid over communicate. An email announcement is a format that sent when no specific response is expected on the part of the recipient; examples include greetings, thank you messages, press releases and order confirmations. Sending these email formats, we will focus on relationship building as opposed to generating immediate sales or leads. Sometimes it's good to receive an email that doesn't ask you to do anything. Email formats are most cffcctive when your email designs and layouts are a good match for the format you choose.

Branding you Business:

You need to pay attention to the way your emails look because your audience pays attention for not depending on the design choices you make any mail. The first rule of email design is that your email designs must be good match with your other marketing media; for example when somebody looks your website and signs up for your email list, they might not recognize your emails, if they totally look different from your site. To make sure a good match between your email designs and your other marketing design, you may follow these guidelines: put your logo in all your emails. Use colors that match your logo for backgrounds borders and set a promotion that suggest the use of colors outside your brand such as running a following promotion with good color. Make sure to work the promotional colors into your brand instead of replacing your brand with the promotion. Also use the same type of images and all your emails; for example there's a big difference between the lookup stock photography and the look of graphics and clipart. Choose the image type that fits the personality of your business and then stick to it. When choosing email designs, it's important to brand each type of email format consistently; for example make sure your email newsletter looks similar but not identical to your email promotions that way people recognize your brand and the purpose of each email. One of the best ways to ensure brand consistency with all your emails is to design your emails based on similar looking email templates.

E-Mail Layout:

Laying out your content in an email usually requires building tables in HTML using cascading style sheets or CSS to tell your recipient's computer how to display your content; not interested in programming your own layout. You can use predesigned email templates that are ready to receive images, links, text, etc. Email templates are available from email marketing providers. Many suppliers include templates that are almost ready to use as well as templates that can be highly customized without any familiarity of HTML language. Content that draws attention to a specific section of your email or call visual anchors as the content works like a newscaster that causes the eyes to stop on content while scanning through the email. Visual newscaster include: headlines, images links, icons, divider lines, background colors and borders.

When put down your content, the most significant content should reside in the upper left quadrant of your email because most people start scanning and emailing the upper left also most mobile devices display emails beginning with the upper left if the whole email doesn't fit on the screen. One word of caution, it's important not to place too many visual newscasters in all four quadrants. It makes your email difficult to scan because the eyes can decide what the most important section of the email is. Organizing your content of columns is another great way to make your email easy to scan and make it easy to organize related groups of content to your audience and can scan each column as if it's a mini account of your email. It has three basic choices for laying out columns effectively in your email: you can use columns of equal width to avoid emphasizing the continent one column over the other. You can put a narrow column on the left side of your email to emphasize the content in a larger column to the right. You can also put a narrow column on the right part of email to highlight the content in a larger column to the left. If you feel like you have so much content a single email that you need to organize your content into more than two columns may want to think flouting up your content into manifold shorter emails and sending with a higher frequency.

Making Your Email Content Valuable:
Include links:

A good test of an effective marketing email is whether or not the email generates immediate sales or move people closer to a purchase decision. In short, your email should invite action and decision making. Events in emails typically engage clicking on links which may include text links, images, buttons and other graphics. Email links are of two varieties: **external web links and internal navigation links**. External links open a browser window of the person who clicks on the link which is directed to a webpage. You can also create links to fills stored on the server and links can open up an email program installed on your subscriber's computer. Emails received on a mobile device could also interpret as a phone number or an address as a link. Phone numbers in the text of your email dial the phone number when hover over & addresses can robotically link to an online map or map application. There is no need to program these types of links. Mobile campaign can identified them automatically. Internal links also known as anchor links point refers to content within the email. You may use internal links to help the person reading your emails to skip to content underneath the display from the peak of the email and hop back to the top of the email from the bottom. You can also use collects of internal links like a table of contents to list the articles or sections of your email allow someone to quickly jump to that section of email without scrolling. When creating text links the best practice is to avoid using the expression 'click here': as the link; as an alternative use an action word or phrase as the link; for example a link to add an item to online shopping may say 'buy the item' instead of "To buy this item, click Here". The more descriptive you may create your text links, the superior possibility you have of inviting click; for example a link that reads more information is not as expressive as a link that studies download the 60 page catalog. When creating image links, the best practices to contain some text in the image appealing the click and explaining what the image link points to. Some images are sensitive as links, so text is a necessary; examples include pictures of products that link to more information about the product, company logos pointing to the homepage of website, audio icons such as a play button that looks like a speaker. Speaking of videos and other files using links to deliver files & videos to email subscribers by no means fix videos, pictures, documents or other files to your email because email filters and bloggers are infamous for banding attachments, bouncing emails with attachments and filtering emails with attachments to junk folder. Creating links and including them in your emails important step toward making actionable emails.

Valuable:

The information you sent an email has to be valuable on a consistent basis or your subscribers will quickly become unsubscribers. While it is good to send bids and inducements to make your emails more valuable, some of your email content needs to be basically precious as well. It is typically only a small portion of your prospects and customers are prepared to purchase when they get one of email. If you limit your email content to promotions and offers, your emails will be immaterial to the bulk of subscribers; some examples of content that can add to the inherent value of your emails. Information about products or services or your company can be valuable especially for new prospects of the people who are interested in learning about new products with the latest trends. Tips and advice can be valuable if purchasing your goods and services engage research, expertise or sound reasoning. Tips and advice can come from you or your employees or you can feature tips and advice from your satisfied customers or product suppliers. Instructions and instructions can tell clients how to get the nearly all out of your products or services before a sale and after a sale. Instructions and directions can also have your customers feel smarter about the purchases they make. Entertaining content can include humor, engaging stories and even professional performances. If you use entertaining content, make sure it has a little to do with purchasing your goods & services otherwise your email subscribers won't be as likely to recall your brand as a source of the content. Facts and researcher are a good idea, when your audience needs more than an opinion to make a purchase decision. Coming up with valuable content can be handled in-house or through external sources such as copywriters and agencies. If you decide to use content from other sources in your email always ask for written permission so you don't violate any copyright laws. Assume all content is copyright protected and consult a licensed attorney if you aren't sure if you have permission to use someone else's content.

Offers:

Valuable offers or incentives help to trounce buy uncertainty and choice evasion. The first rule of valuable offers is to know your customers because diverse groups of people may react in a different way to the same offers; for example some people love to know about discounted product because they like to save money. However some people associate the word discount with words like cease, despicable or out of style. At most these two groups of people require very different offers; the former may respond completely to an email broadcasting an auction while the latter is more likely to value an email announcing a sneak sample of the newest & most luxurious produce line. For the best results conduct a survey or watch your email tracking account to find out what subscriber's value then split your email list and groups based on the types of offers that motivate each group. Coupons included in an email can be printed out or shown on a mobile device for in-store redemption or link to an item in an online store. Use coupons when your prospects or customers want to be rewarded with prices that are available to the general public. To add a personal touch to your email coupons are a mail merge include your subscribers name on the coupon. Giveaways or free products or services offered in exchange for information or purchase. Use giveaways in combination with another product purchase when you want to offer more value without discounting the value of the featured product; for example if a car dealer offered a car at 50% off people might wonder what's wrong with the car. If however the car was offered at full price with a giveaway worth 50% of the value of the car, the same values proceed without discounting the car. If you decide to offer giveaways, make sure to check your local laws to make sure your giveaway doesn't qualify as a sweepstakes contest or lottery; if it does need to comply with local laws for these types of promotions. Lost leaders are another form of giveaway a loss leader is a promotional price; they results in a loss to the business when the products purchased. Why would you offer a product in an email at a price that waste money because you want to acquire a new customer with an extremely low price? So you can realize profits through repeat sales generated by additional emails after the initial loss leader purchase. Use lost leaders when you want to attract new customers to your business and away from the competition. Once you have an offer that gets people to react it's time to assist them get the next step by signifying one or more actions that's called a call to action.

Call to Act:

A call to action is a statement of promise your audience to take one or more specific actions in favor of your purposes. Calling for act is not as easy as including a phone number in your emails or giving people lots of links to click on. You need to give people a few hints of you know exactly what you want to do. Contrary to what you observe in a large number of emails 'Click Here' is not the best way to call for action in the email. Instead of 'Click Here' begin your call to action with a word that explain the action; examples include visit, call, download, read or print. You can turn your call to action statements in the links or combined with phone numbers or specific instructions. Sometimes, the main reason the call for action is to ask for immediate purchase. There are lots of other reasons to include a call to action in your email; for example you can use a call to action to request people to read your email by starting your email with a statement like read this email before you buy online. You can also use a call to action to highlight a specific portion of your email as in the statement: scroll down for a valuable coupon. Sometimes it's appropriate to ask people to save your email for later instead of deleting it if they are ready to take advantage of offering your email. You can also ask people to show the email by printing it out or showing emaill on a mobile device and don't forget to ask people to share your email with a friend or colleague when I finally found content of value to someone we care about. You may decide to focus on one called action in your email but sometimes including multiple calls to action. One email can actually increase the number of responses you get. One of the best ways to increase responses using multiple calls to action is asked for three different levels of promise from your readers. For example a chocolate company might send an email promoting a new gift basket with the following three calls to action: order this gift basket today, download or gift basket catalog and like this gift basket on Facebook. Each of these calls to action results in a positive action even if the person reading the email isn't interested in making a purchase right away.

From:

Creating a familiar front line is critical to getting your emails opened and read because people don't like to receive emails unless they know the sender; especially when it comes from a business. Unfamiliar email from lies can also result in spam complaints; even when people explicitly signed up for your email list; just because they don't know you. To make you once familiar ask your customers how know you which include that information front line. If you or your employees have personal relationships with your customers use your first and last names in front lines. If your business is a local branch of the larger organization, make sure you're from line includes your location to differentiate your emails from the other branches in the main corporate emails. If your business uses an acronym such as ABC Company make sure your customers also know you by your acronym; otherwise it's best to use your full business name. It's also important to make your email address familiar; for example the ABC Company could send their newsletters from the email address newsletter@company.com.

Subject Line:

Your subject line is the part of your email that prompts your recipients to hopefully open your email and start reading immediately. Subject lines get stop after about 50 or 60 characters; so the best way to utilize the subject line of email is to describe the instant benefit of opportunity your email with the fewest words possible; Subject lines such as July newsletter from a company may be too general and are not strong enough to prompt an immediate open. Instead of general words choose worthy words for your focus lines. Value words are words or phrases that describe the benefit readers will get by creating the email. Few examples are; if the benefit of your email as financial investments you may employ the word savings as the rated word in your subject line as in over $50 in savings in this email. To the benefit of your email is valuable information you should use words in your subject line that describe the immediate benefit of reading your information. For example; if your information helps someone to compare the competition your subject line may read compare the competition under two minutes. If the benefit of opening your emails is basically the same in a series of emails you can work off the theme by creating a brand for your emails and including a brand name as the subject line. For example, instead of using the word newsletter in the subject line for every newsletter you send, you can create a name for your newsletter such as smart shopper weekly of your retail store or five-minute sales tips if you offer sales consulting. Coming up with good subject lines consistently is not easy; if you're unsure about whether a particular idea for subject line work. Try testing one idea for subject line against another idea using a small sample of your email list. Remember also to avoid subject lines that look like spam. Using all capital letters excessive punctuation were extreme urgency off putting and cause spam complaints. Take a few minutes to periodically check your own junk or spam folder to see what the spammers are using in their subject lines and then avoid copying their techniques.

Social Feature:

Emails can be forwarded shared, liked, tweeted, rated and reviewed. You can use basic social media features to endorse your social media item to email subscribers and you can use more advanced social media features to allow your social media followers to use your emails without receiving them in an email inbox.

To promote your social media content your email subscribers, simply include links to your social media sites in the body of your emails; for example you may want to add Facebook icon to your email; linked to your business page on Facebook. Posting your email to social sites is simple through email marketing gateway; because they can automatically send your email inboxes, Facebook & Twitter when you plan your email to go out. That way you create email content once and publishers everywhere is one campaign. When it comes to publishing your emails to multiple places, don't forget to include mobile devices.

Mobile Friendly:

Lots of people check and read their emails on mobile devices such as smart phones and tablet devices. So it's important to consider these devices when creating marketing emails; specifically there are three things to consider when you send email to people who are likely to read them on mobile devices: firstly most people admit the email inbox with smart phones tablets and computers. So you shouldn't design emails for smart phones without thinking about how the designs will work on computers and tablets; second is the usefulness of your email content to a personal mobile device. When people using mobile devices to read email the more likely to be sorting through emails and deciding what to open now save for later what to delete immediately. The more useful your email is in a mobile context more likely your email will be opened immediately or save for later use; for example if your email contains a coupon that the recipient can show in a store to receive a discount it's more useful in a mobile context than an email that ask your recipient to go through an online order process involves a lot of typing. It may be easier on a computer keyboard. Thirdly how the email will be appeared and function on a mobile device. Smart phones have much smaller screens and computers is often frustrating for people to scroll around to find links text and images. The most effective mobile email designs take advantage of the upper left portion of the email; that's because most mobile devices either display emails beginning with the upper left portion of the email or the display of the whole width of the email on the screen requiring the recipient to zoom and scroll to specific sections of email. When people zoom and scroll they often start in the upper left of the email; at least in countries where people read from left to right. You can place business logo or business name in the upper left; you can begin your email message with the main headline at the top of your email. Images in the upper left can be effective to but you might want to make sure it's small enough for some text to fit next to it were below it to encourage people to scroll. You can place navigation links in the upper left so people can quickly scroll and click to the content in your email or onto a website. Remember that direction-finding links are essential only when email has lots of content to your audience has to scroll to view. If you decide you require a table of contents as the amount of content in your email is so large then take a moment to think about whether you're sending too much information in single email? In the first place cutting down your content and increasing your frequency might be a better solution to making your emails easier to navigate our mobile screen.

Mobile Calls:

When people read your emails on mobile devices they are more likely to respond if you include a call to act that makes it easy or more attractive for people to take action using the device. Hear some of the capabilities to give mobile email so much potential. Smart phones allow people to touch or click on a phone number to immediately; include your phone number in your emails to make it easy for people to contact you. Some smart phones and other mobile devices also allow an address to automatically link to maps and directions. So, include your present address in your mail if you have one or more physical locations. For including links to your website to optimize your website pages. Mobile web pages have simplified navigation and content it easier to read on smaller screens. A good web designer can help you to detect mobile device visitors and serve up a version of your website such friendly to each type of device. Links to videos also work well in smart phones and mobile devices. For the best result poster videos to public sites such as YouTube to make sure your videos will play on all types of devices. In addition to links in your email content you can also use your email content to suggest mobile friendly actions; such as taking a picture and attaching it when replying to your email, visiting a social media site to follow your business, write a review, checking into a location on a check insight like foursquare, Facebook or showing the email to someone else. Showing an email works great for coupons another offers in your email if you have a retail store; because you can tell people to show the email to a company representative to receive the discount will be offer mentioned in email. Mobile technology is rapidly advancing.

Maximizing Email Campaign:
Blocked Mail:

Email isn't delivered hundred percent of the time but undelivered email isn't necessarily void of opportunity. Bouncing blocked emails are returned to the email senders email address with code to tells you why the email was blocked. Of course email servers are exactly have a way with words so I recommend using an email service provider that can classify your bouncing block emails and reports that are easier for humans to interpret. Bounce reports show you which email bounce and why they bounced so that you can take the appropriate action. Emails that are permanently undeliverable called **Hard Bounced**. Hard bounce means that the email address does not exist so it's either misspell, the addresses been changed or been abandoned by the owner. When you see a hard bounce in your bounce report you should either contact your subscribers via another method to obtain a new email address or simply delete them from your database. When your email bounce report shows an email return as mailbox full, temporarily undeliverable or blocked these situations are known as **Soft Bounces**. Soft bounces may be temporary or permanent so check your bounce report to see how often a particular email is bounced. If you notice three or more consecutive soft bounces for an email address should treat it just like a hard bounce. If you notice the regular soft bounces, you can try resetting your emails later date. Remember the best way to reduce blocked emails is to make sure your email list is up-to-date in the first place. Send an email once every three months or so reminding your subscribers to notify you or update your subscription profile if they change email addresses; that way to better chance of catching some of the email address changes before they show up one of bounce report. Another preventative measure is avoiding email filters that deliver your email to junk and spam folders instead of bouncing emails back as undeliverable.

Reduce Filter:

Email filters are always negative. Some people set up filters to sort emails into different folders to keep your emails organize. The filters you want to avoid are the types that sort emails into a junk or spam folder. Many junk filters are put by users to block attachment, profanity or specific senders. But most filters are set by email companies who want protect their customers from malicious content, spam and other unwanted emails. You should first make sure your email items for anything that shares the characteristics of a typical spam email; examples include subject lines with capital letters, attachment & profanity or certain words that are common in spam emails. Spam emails & legitimate emails often split alike individuality; so I recommend using an email service provider with a spam make sure feature that scans the content of email for spam like content. You don't use an email service provider with a spam check feature. Verify your junk or spam folder once in a while to see what techniques the spammers are using to get there emails delivered and then avoid copying those tactics in your own emails. Avoiding spam like content is an important part of avoiding filters; but it's even more important to make sure you establish a good sender reputation with email companies like Yahoo, Gmail, Hotmail and AOL. Your sender reputation is made up of three things: the length of time you have been transferring email from a specific server; the number of emails you sent from a particular server and the number of spam complaints you received from your subscribers. One of the best ways to make sure your sender reputation is well-established, is to use a well-established email service provider to send your emails on your behalf; email service providers with recognized reputation have produced their reputations through close working relationships with the email companies and by sending high volumes of emails to permission-based lists. We sign up for an email service you also sign-up to adhere to their best practices and permission policies. So make sure your email list is permission-based compliant with all of the email service providers policies before you sign up and pay for a subscription or software package.

Open Click:

Email marketing doesn't end and when your email gets delivered; in fact that's when things really start to get interesting. Email tracking requires some serious HTML programming or you may use a mail marketing provider with built in tracking and reporting to show you who is opening clicking on your emails. Once you have following potential in your emails you need to understand; what it means when your reports show, opens and clicks and opened email according to an email tracking report means that the person who received the email enable the images in the email to display or clicking a link in the email. No images, no open counted on the tracking report; this is important to understand because a lot of people reading emails without enabling the images were clicking on any links. Your open rate is a guide to see how many people were interested enough in a particular email to enable the images were click a link and then assume the people who were not listed in your open report noticed your email and just chose to scan the email content without clicking or enabling and images. When it comes to your click report, things are a lot more straightforward. Your click report shows who clicks on which links and how many people clicked on each link. Your click report gives you two great insights. First, clicks are indications of interest on the part of your email subscribers; for example if 20 people click on a link to watch a video about dogs and 20 people click a link to watch a video about cats. You can determine which people are interested in dogs and which are interested in cats; that way the next series of emails you sent can be customized further the dog people or cat people. Secondly, click report also tells whether email content is valuable and interesting to your readers. When people click to view website read an article watch a video or download a picture they are engaging and that helps them to remember your business and your message when the ready to buy; For this reason it's a good idea to leave some of your email content out of your email and link it instead; that way you can tell who's interested and who is not. When analyzing your click report it's also a good idea to compare your email data with your website visitor data. If your email brings a lot of traffic to site but no one takes any action from their communication it is an indication that your website content or your user experience may be in need.

Track Non Click:

Email links the drive traffic to a website can be tracked electronically but non-click responses have to be tracked with little human interaction and creativity. Here are the non-click responses that are worth tracking. Firstly, it is a fine thought to track store purchases ensuing from your emails, if you have a physical store. To track store purchase ask people to your mail either by printing it out or showing it on mobile device screen. You can also track store purchases by counting a special promotion that is advertise anywhere except your emails that way when anyone asks for the particular endorsement. You know the only way they found out about it was through one of emails. Including a particular endorsement also works well if you track phone calls generated from your emails because you can attribute any caller to mention the special offer to your emails. You can take the concept one step further by a unique phone number in emails so that anyone who calls the number is identified as someone who received an email.

Another non-click response worth tracking is event attendance; of course you can track event registrations electronically. But sometimes it's good to know how many reminders an invitation emails contributed to increasing actual physical attendance; especially if your events are free. In the case of events you can use your emails us tickets and you can ask people to show or print the emails for admission or you can include offers in your reminder emails that people can show or mention of the door. If the fact that tracking non-click responses require some manual intervention has you worried about spending too much time; don't worry.

Email Automation:

One of the best benefits of mail marketing is the aptitude to automate marketing communications. You need an email marketing provider or really good programmer to help you with email automation. Few automation scenarios are simple and some are simple conceptually; but they're very complicated technically. The first type of email automation is called an auto responder. Auto responder is a single email sent automatically in response to a specific event or action; examples an email triggered by a precise date such as a birthday holiday or calendar date; an email triggered by a precise time such as mealtime or some hours before an event. An email sent in response to filling out a form such as order or joining an email list or an email sent in response to a click; such as a click on a link to a website page or a video. To setup up an auto-responder you need to create an email with content that is same for everybody who triggers the autoresponder email. What you created email, you can use your email marketing provider to assign it to one or more triggers were events. Sometimes it's appropriate to send multiple emails automatically in response to action or event. An automated series of multiple emails is called the sequence. Sequences are perfect for targeting email content to individuals with different behaviors interests or contents; for example when a new prospect jointer email list you may want to set up a sequence that automatic response with the following four emails. A welcome email thanking the person for joining the email list was sent immediately after joining. A follow-up email with links to a product catalog company information or other helpful resources, sent three days after the welcome email. An email newsletter with articles and recommendation sent one week after the follow-up email and a promotional email offering a special discount as a thank you for joining the email list sent two weeks after the email newsletter. Sequences create your emails more applicable as you can base them on a variety of relevant events and triggers; such as clicks date & period of time since a previous action when it comes to planning more sophisticated email sequences, you'll even email marketing provider that has the ability to automatically stop or change a sequence based on multiple trigger; for example to create a sequence for new prospects and what was new prospects becomes a customer in the middle of your new prospects sequence you may want to switch that person to a new customer sequence and stop the new prospects sequence. To automate sequence changes, your email marketing provider needs to integrate with your database and link tracking to identify changes in a customer profile so switching someone from one sequence to another may be as simple as permitting to track clicks or purchase and adjust each sequence accordingly. You can also manually add someone to a sequence more stop a sequence by changing the data in someone's database record email automation takes a little extra time to set up.

CHAPTER 7
BLOGGING MARKETING

Blogging can be a useful tool in the marketing strategy of any business and the right you can also turn into a convention point amid the industry and its customers. Throughout the book, we will go through five stages that will help you lay the groundwork to get from the idea of a business blog to an actual live in functioning blog to make it more effective. First, look at how to define goals and expectations and established timeline to meet these goals then we'll discuss strategy both for content creation and marketing and how to measure success. We will look at technology choices and how these affect our blog and can be used to further its functionality. We will take a deep dive into content creation and look at how to manage a blog and produce excellence content by influencing the trust in your business and finally look at how to incorporate an existing corporate identity and plan the publication on the blog. Of this blog can be a powerful addition to your online marketing package. By establishing obvious goal & a plan creating value, a business blog become the face of your business to the all-white community.

Blogging for Business:

What is a blog?:

You may be attended to many different contingent understandings and you probably also have your own understanding of what a blog is and what work means? Let's take a look at the word blog where it came from, what is used to mean and what it means today and based on that make a definition we could use as a basis for our projects. The first person to use the word blog was Peter Myrtles. This was back in 1999 and he derived it from the longer weblog which was coined by John Barger in 1997. Back then a weblog or blog was basically an online life log or journal. That's pretty close to the unique meaning of a blog. From the Merriam Webster dictionary, "a blog website that contains an online personal journal with reflection, remarks & frequently hyperlinks provided by the writer". In other words blogs were identified by common elements such as a reverse chronological stream or blog posts with the most recent polls displaying the top, a sidebar with links to blogger archives, categories, blog roll of links to other blogs and comment sections for each individual posts. That was then; today the definition of a blog has evolved along with the medium of the web to mean something somewhat different. If you ask your friend on Google, a blog is a website on which an individual or group of user record view in order etc on a usual basis. This much broader definition not only fits with how the web and blogs themselves are used today but also shows how blogs have infringed on the previously clearly defined territory of the website to become a subset rather than an alternative. The key to this modern definition is that tail end of the definition on a regular basis and this is what sets of blog apart from a website. A website generally consists of a defined number of pages and sub pages that are presented in more or less static formats. Only rarely are new pages added to the websites. The blog on the other hand, is a constant source of new information and its use to push this information out to the public and engage the public. To put in business terms, the website is the annual statements; the blog is a newsletter but almost a newsletter the blog and its contents is usually created to appeal to a wider audience as part of the overall marketing plan for the business. In short, for business the blog is a platform through which customers and the general public can be reached and engaged.

Why Blogging is required?

A blog is a website on which an individual or group of users record opinions, information etc on a regular basis what is the value in blogging for business? Should not the opinions and information about a business be hosted on a cautiously forbidden website? The answer is yes. The opinions and information about a business should be hosted on website. The blog comes in addition and will serve as a platform to communicate a different type of opinions and information. The reasons for the explosive popularity and growth of blogs are that they made distribution opinion & thoughts easier than ever. The blogging tools and platforms remove the requirements to appreciate web servers & programming languages to issue content on the web and serve as intermediaries between people and the web and once people share their opinion and ideas freely, others took these ideas and share them with their group of friends and so on; and the reason why people were so eager to share this content was because it was a different type of content from one regular old websites provided. Blogs were full of tips and tricks ideas and concepts debates and creativity and that's the type of content the people of the web model new ones but also want to share. For business, this distinction can be hard to grasp once it's properly understood and implemented; it is an invaluable asset for brand awareness, marketing and communication with existing and potential customers. The key to great blog is to share precious imminent and in order with the world. Back and come in the form of tutorials, articles, opinion, piece, question & answers the list goes on and if a blog does this and does it well it can easily become a trusted source of information for both your customers and for search engines. The web has become an integrated entity; everything is linked together. And by understanding and tapping into this integration, good blogging strategy can have a positive impact on the business website as a whole. For business the point of a blog is to share valuable insights and information not only about its own products but also about the general business landscape. This will return in a higher trust and share factor among the web by community which in turn means higher search rankings on search engines for the blog and for the website. The end results is better brand awareness; the website, the blog and social media platforms join together to form the face of the industry online and the blog is what ties it all together.

Stages of Blogging

We will follow a game plan that has five main stages and at each stage will define the parameters that the end of the course will become the baseline elements for your business blog. The first stage focuses on setting goals for the blog. These goals will be based on the goals for the business as a whole and are created to help focus the blog and ensure that all online and marketing assets are aiming towards the same target. In the second stage, we look at strategy and will discuss the positioning of the blog in relation to other online and off-line assets management and decision-making structure of the blog itself and who has publishing rights and final say. It will also look at how the success of the blog will be measured against the goals for the blog and for the business. The third stage looks at technology; because of the prevalence and popularity of blogs, there are many different platforms to choose from each with their own benefits and drawbacks and the plat from you select will have a significant impact on the blog you end up publishing. There is also a plethora of three and 4 services available online; that can augments plug into and work next to your blog to enlarge its digital footprints on the web. We will discuss these technologies and I'll help you make an informed decision in a strategy for how to implement them for the best results. In the fourth stage, look at content creation. How to define what type of content should be published on the blog, who should create and manage this contents and how the content should be published for the most impact and bang for your buck. The fifth and final stage is implementation. This is where the different segments come together and the blog itself take shape. With all the previous stage is complete you'll have a clear path to follow when decisions about the sign publishing schedules and social interaction need to be made and you'll be ready to create publish and manage a blog for your business. It may seem like an elaborate process just to make a blog but trust me it pays off in spades at the end. Before publishing has always been a great strategy and what it comes to blogging for business the more planning perceives the publishing the better.

Define your Goal:

The first and most important step in creating a business blog is to define clear goals for the blog. This also happens to be the most unnoticed part of the planning process and for good reason. Defining goals for something that just looks similar to chance update concerning industry related items seems unnecessary. But just like with business itself if the blog doesn't have clear goals will be left flailing with no clear focus or intends. Defining clear goals for your blog will help in two ways; firstly you will set targets for everyone who works with the blog; second you may use these to measure your success. In answering the question how you define goals for a blog while first you have to establish the goal, the blog will support the business; so dear goals should be in line with each other. So, let's look at the goals for the business itself to find out how blogging can help a business. First stage of the process is the goal section which comes with the first reference card. The first section of the goals card is the business purpose this is where you need to structure of your business. The best place to start this process is by talking to the people at the center of it the entire top of the pyramid owners and executives and also the marketing department. The core purpose of the business. This is often confused with a mission statement or corporate timeline that these are usually far too vague and inspirational; what you want? What should go on card to raw purpose of the business? What is its essence; for our example the business purpose is to sell clean energy products so that's what goes on the card. Sell clean energy products when you establish this business purpose. You can take a look at all the activities in your business and see how they are or at least how they should be furthering the key goal. Asking questions like why do we publicize educational materials or white us provide our employees with on-the-job training? The answer will always be some form of this business purpose? We publicize educational materials to educate people so they find reasons to buy our clean energy products. We provide employees with on-the-job training so they are better equipped to sell clean energy products the same goals for the blog why do we have a blog? The market the company and as a result sell more clean energy products. Clearly defining and spelling out the business purpose prime objectives or goal for business has benefits that reach far beyond the pond will blog. It also provides a new and welcome perspective on the business itself. Simply put stating out loud what you actually do will help you do it better.

Objectives:

With the business purpose clearly recognized and printed down on the goals card, you're ready to start finding specific and possible goals for the blog. The key is to always ensure the goals of the blog lineup for the business purpose of the company. To get this process started brainstorming topics about how you want to communicate, what the business does, to the web using public. Here, is important to remember what a blog is; a sharing and communication platform. Therefore questions to start brainstorming sessions should point towards active and participatory elements. What can a blog visitor learn from us? What to do once to learn from us? What can we learn from our customers? How can we contribute to debate in the field? How do we establish ourselves as thought leaders? Let's look at our example; what in a blog visitor learn. We can educate them on green technology; whatever the business purpose of your company the answers to these types of questions should always be followed by the question how can this be used to get us closer to your business purpose. This question leads to our goal so in our example, the goal would be become a leading resource on information about green technologies. In other words the goals for the blog focus on sharing ideas and becoming a trusted resource while in game is to drive customers to do business. Let's take a look at the other questions what do they want to learn from us? When we get lots of inquiries we don't currently have a database of frequently asked questions. So, the goal would be reached out to potential and existing customers to help create an FAQ on RT technology fields. What can we learn from our customers? Several customers have shared their success stories about implementing or technologies with us; so the goal here would be share customer stories and insights to encourage file sharing. You can also define both short-term and long-term goals for the blog as in this example; how can we contribute to the debate in our field and establish ourselves as thought leaders. Our staffers are experts on solar energy. They can pipe in on political decisions around this topic by sharing the 14th of facts and figures and technical know-how. So the short-term goal in this case is become a goal to source of information about solar energy for news publications; while the long-term goal may be shape political opinion about solar energy. These goals will help focus the content of your blog and ensure them what is published is in line with the overall business purpose of your company. The goals you end up defining will be asking your business.

Plan Properly:

Welcome goals is liked and it's equally important to set specific goals approximately rising readership interchange and appointment. I advocate creating a one year plan with milestones so everyone working on the blog will know what they are functioning towards and how to measure success as they move forward. The goals card will help to set up a one year timeline and put incremental milestones for the foreseeable future blog. When you create your one year plan, it is important to set practical outlook and to do so we first have to understand how the blog will function in the larger context of online by persons of the company. The web is overflowing the blogs so rarely publishing a blog and expecting it to start carrying in readers is not realistic. To get eyes on the blog you have to invest time, money marketing and engagement and here as in most etc. The return of investments is proportionate to the investment itself. The first milestone over card for the first week of the blog is about building immediate interest; that could mean getting the blog mentioned in a newsletter or an industry publication or even holds the launch party. Search engines like blogs; as they are continuously updated and because their contents is more purely based search engines also rank blogs supported on how well they ask and answer questions whether people find trustworthy and easy way to bolster this is a publish customer testimonials and stories were off her up best practice examples to answer clone questions or challenges customers may face. The second milestone on a card for the first month is about publishing search friendly contents; as an example it could be published five customer stories or publish the answers to common questions. A blog is an organic part of your overall marketing and branding strategy for business. This means the optimistic power of the blog does not come exclusively in the form of direct visits to the blog; it also comes from how the blog content is shared on the web and how help people start seeing the content in the company came from as a valued resource. The third milestone over card at month three is to boost visits to the blog of the main website through social media; an example would be double visitor numbers or month-to-month basis. Once your blog is starting to get traction in search and social media it's important to own a mobile type of content people are searching for and sharing & rising manufacture and publication of that type contents. It also turns out that the type of content using people once in the title content people actually want wildly different things. The fourth milestone at the six-month mark is about evaluation; for example identify the three most found and shared articles on the blog to be used as content templates for future posts. The fifth milestone at the nine-month mark is a direct follow-up using the data from the six-month mark to run experiments on targeted content production; tripled direct search hits and shares the polls based on contents templates. The sixth and last milestone up to 12 months mark is a revisit and reset. For the first year of the blog my recommendation is to not set specific expectations but rather establish a baseline for future operations. It takes time for a blog to establish itself on web and this time can be used to gather metrics about visitor performance and communication as well as testing with different publishing models. At the one-year mark you can look at all the data you have composed and recognize what works and what doesn't work and what can be improved upon. With this in mind you can go back to the first stage go through the entire process again from goals all the way to completion and return to every choice to see if it needs to be revised. A blog like the web has to be a moving target and by making yearly revisit every aspect of the planning process you create an agile process that allows the blog to evolve with the times.

Strategy:

The question where does the blog live might seem a little showing. It lives on the web on the server most likely on your server. It is not what I mean; when asked the question? what I mean is where does the blog live in family member to your other online possessions. This is an important question to answer early in the planning process. Depending on what type of business you're working for and how the business uses the web the positioning of the blog will vary much. The reason you desire to believe this through and make a decision about the positioning of the blog is that will impact how you handle your online assets in the future and it will also impact how the consumers and customers interact with the same assets. We now moving to the strategy section where we find the strategy card; the front page of the plan card will be used to sketch a map of all your online assets and how they relate to one another. The most excellent way to get a grip on your online possessions and how they interact is to place them on a map and draw arrows between this. This can be done on a sketch or on a whiteboard or even using individual cutout pieces for each asset; when you want to do is identify each asset; so your main websites and intranets, the customer portal your Twitter version and Facebook & any other assets run by the company. Once you have all their assets on the board start drawing arrows between them to shoulder current relationship with each other. If your main website has twitter link on, use an arrow from the site to twitter. If your website has a YouTube video on it, use an arrow pointing from you to your website. You get the idea. Now, the blog into the mix either with a different color or on different draw. Think about where the blog is positioned either inside of the website or outside and how the blog changes the connecting between elements. Blog can be built around a looser information philosophy incorporating elements from social media like tweets and Facebook updates & implanting YouTube videos etc. The blog can also be used to point the visitor directly at key possessions on the major website while at the same time adding more information to the discussion or it can be used as the admission between the industry & social media in general. Once you have a clear picture of all your assets and how they relate to one another drawing on the front of the strategy card.

Owns:

If you think about it a blog is a lot like a newspaper or magazine. You constantly publish new content and you have multiple authors and contributors to create this content and just like a newspaper or magazine you need to have an editorial hierarchy with clearly defined roles so everyone working on the blog knows the answer to and find that the editorial decisions are consistent and in line with the overall company policies. On the strategic card, you have an editorial map. Before we move on we need to fill in this map putting a name to each of the tears and ensuring that the roles and responsibilities for each of these tears are clearly defined. At the top, find editor-in-chief; this person is the de facto owner of the blog and is the person answers for its contents. The editor in chief has final say on what gets published and he/she is responsible for ensuring that all substance is in line with business and blog policies and goals. Finally she makes sure that the tone & appearance of the content is right. The second tier is the content manager responsible for finding and commissioning content for all or a subgroup of topics. The content manager would answer to the editor-in-chief and serve as a strain for her. Third tier is the content editor; responsible for receiving and editing content before it arrives at the content manager. The fourth tier is the contributor. This is a tier in which the content itself was produced previous to being sent to the content editor. This tier will differ depending on the size of your company. For small company one or two people can complete this role but for a large company it can be a good idea to distribute roles. In a real life situation the structure would work something like this. The editor in chief could call for content; the content manager find the right person in the company produces content; the contributor would produce the contents; the content editor would handle cleanups, revisions and rewrites; the content manager would look over the content making sure it's in line with what was specially made and finally the editor-in-chief receives the contents checks to confirming it's in line with objectives & rules and tells the content manager to publish it to the blog. The reason for this structure is to make sure there is oversight at each stage in the process by clearly defining roles it will diminish the load on a single person by handing out liability across the different tiers and yes as you can see this essentially means there will be a person in your business whose major focus or sole job is to be the editor-in-chief owner of the blog.

Guidelines:

Creating editorial guidelines for business blog will help you set the framework for content production. It will also give both content makers and the appointments public a clear understanding of what can be expected from the blog. With the cards and information you've collected so far you can establish a comprehensive set of editorial guidelines to get editors, contributors and visitors a clear picture of what they can expect to what is expected of them. To help start this process, we have created an editorial guidelines template. This is not complete and depending on your particular state of affairs and supplies you can add or take away basics and change anything in the guidelines to fit your particular business blog. At the core of editorial guidelines lie two key components. The list of editorial staff in the principles of publishing; your established a list of editorial staff of the strategy card; this list should be added to the editorial guidelines to make it clear to everyone who holds the key roles and responsibilities for publishing the blog and its content is worried. This list will be updated whenever there's a change in editorial staff. The principles of publishing outline the overall principles the blog adheres to. Here you should list the principles and philosophies of the company itself and also principles of editorial and journalistic ethics. By publishing content you are taking part in an age old tradition of in order sharing and it's vitally important but you establish and adhere to a strict code of principles when it approaches for publishing this information. This includes being open and honest about your association, being truthful and correcting your mistake because you publishing content online in a social media setting there also some other issues to consider. These should be at the foundation of all content creation the entire web and I encourage you to read through and incorporate them into your editorial guidelines. The rest of the guidelines are self-explanatory; set out guidelines for the type of content to be published and how specific elements are handled including images, links & content from outside sources. The editorial rules are in many ways a legal documents and it's important to include organization, lawful and advertising in the endorsement process of the guidelines. Once the editorial guidelines have been finished and approved give them to everybody in the editorial staff or contributors and other asset holders posted up an office and share all the blog itself to ensure complete transparency.

Technology:

When publishing a blog or any other type of content on the web, it is important to understand how the web works and how people can interact with this content. Let's first look at webpage mechanism. A server is connected to the web; almost server there's a web documents. You can open that web documents using a web browser and see its contents. In the scenario each new webpage is a new web document ; simple buy when there's a lot of pages or you once advanced interactive components like remarking it gets tricky. Enter content management system. A CMS allows you to use templates and a database to populate the pages that means instead of having a web server with one document for each page; you have a web server with template files in a database and then the CMS takes the appropriate template files and combined them with the appropriate database content to create the page in the visiting browser. The advantage of the CMS is that the stream of information can also leave in the other way; the user or administrator can enter information on a webpage that is sent back to the database. This is how blogs work because blogging applications are simplified content management systems. When you pick what blogging application you want to choose, you have two main options : cloud hosted services or self hosting Applications. Cloud hosted services are free or for pay solutions were the server side or back end is handled by a third party and is more or less invisible to you. You send information into the cloud and information comes out of the club; self hosting applications that you place on your own server and manage yourself; their benefits and drawbacks to both which will touch on later in this course. Web publishing today goes beyond the simple publishing pages online. It also includes sharing through social media and social networks. Whenever a new post was published on your blog, it can be linked to and republished throughout social networks to bring attention and readers back to the block. This sharing cycle has become as important if not even more important than search engine results because it's powered by people. Once a pollster's shared on twitter or Facebook or Google plus, it's more likely to be shared on one of the other services as well and the more it's shared on different sites the more attention it will get. Knowing this you need to make sure your chosen blogging platform and infrastructure give you the level of control you need enables sharing across social networks and services and allows you to customize the metadata but it's shared on social networks.

Platforms:

We now move on to the technology section where we refined technology card. This is where you make the important decisions on what platform to baser business blog on and also what technologies and services to hook into for added contact and communication. The first thing you require to make a decision on is the blogging platform; while there are many platforms obtainable we can thin the list down significantly by including in factors like support, prevalence and how often the application is efficient. The least labor-intensive option is WordPress.com a cloud-based service with a free and for pay options; because of the cloud-based service you have limited control over styling and functionality but in return you don't have to be anxious about safety and upgrade. WordPress.com is power-driven by WordPress the most popular and prevalent blogging and content management system on the web today and it's old and operated by a company called automatic; which in turn is run by Matt Mullen quite the cocreator of WordPress itself. WordPress.com is a great option if you want to hand off maintenance and control to third-party. Before most businesses a self hosted solution is to be preferred. For self hosting you have many options but the three most prevalent WordPress, Drupal and Joomla. These are applications you install and run on your own server that can power a blog or website. WordPress is by far the most popular of the three and the application powers close to 20% of all websites worldwide. Its appeal is a simple and intuitive user interface and accessible development platform making it a favorite amongst web designers and developers as well as bloggers. Wordpress is also my chosen platform for blogging and web publishing in general; while Wordpress has grown from a blogging platform into CMS. Drupal and Joomla always been CMS is we blogging functionality built-in. This means those are more complex and have more advanced features under the flood but without added complexity. Whether you choose a solution like WordPress or you want to go with a full CMS like Drupal or Joomla depends in large part on what else you want to do with the solution. If you're just setting up a blog or making a small-scale website WordPress is usually the right solution. If you're looking for enterprise scale platform to handle all your online assets and replace your business website Drupal or Joomla may be better options. Once you selected what blogging platform you want to use highlighted on the card and contact a professional developers specializing in platform to ensure you get it set up correctly.

Social Media:

Once you've picked the blogging platform, you should also consider what social media services you want to use and integrate with. There many options in which services you choose to go with will depend on your target market as well as your budget. A Facebook page is a sound investment for any company that targets the average consumer and Facebook pages can also easily be integrated with blocks. Twitter is a great tool to gather information and interact with the standard consumer but it needs a lot of work to maintain a popular twitter profile. Many companies have a twitter handle mostly to address client question and complaints and this is a bare minimum in my opinion. Google plus is a bit of an unknown of moments. You can choose to treat it like Facebook by setting up a company page and outline or you can decide to use it a small like twitter or conversational basis. The one thing to remember with Google plus is to put up Google plus authorship for blog and its authors so the content gets linked together on Google. YouTube has turn into a search engine of sorts and if you're ready to invest in video production, setting up a YouTube channel and publishing relevant video material can be a great marketing tool; just remember that YouTube is populated by some less than serious elements there is also several other social media and social publishing platforms worth considering including pinterest, LinkedIn. Which social sharing services you choose to invest in will depend on where your target audiences and how they use it. If you have highly shareable content that appeals to the general public, Facebook, Twitter and pinterest may be good focus areas. If your content is more professional in nature linkedin may be a better option. When selecting what social platforms to focus on talk to the marketing department and find out what platforms are already included in the online marketing strategy of the company. Once you pick the platforms highlight them on your part.

Wiredin:

In addition to selecting a blogging platform and social media focus, you'll benefit from integrating common web services. These range from monitoring and analytics to backup and security. Together to ensure a dependable and expectantly trouble-free knowledge for you as the administrator and for the visitor. To key services every website and blog must be link to Google Webmasters and Bing Webmaster tools. These services provided by the two largest search engines on the web check your site for activity. Ensure that your content is indexed properly so people can find it in social search results and also alerts you if and when something goes wrong. Both services are free and easy to set up and the information you get in return is invaluable, when you want to improve your site or learn why it's not working correctly or not being indexed. To get the full benefit out of these Webmaster tools, it's essential to set up comprehensive site map files. This can usually be done automatically through plug-ins or modules for your chosen platforms. Google also has a long list of other free services worth setting up including Google analytics which run statistics on your visitors and how they interact with your site. Google places which associates your website and Google account with the physical location of your business and allows for your website to show up in geographically weighted searches and Google plus authorship which associates individual blog offers with publish contents as well as the blog and site itself. In addition to these services gather information about your sites; you should also invest in services that ensure that everything works properly on your site. This includes proper backup and restoration in case the server crash or malicious attack and security monitoring of your sites. There many different service providers who offer these types of services and you may already have such services internally in your company or integrated into the existing company website. The key here is to ensure you have proper backup routines in place and that someone is making sure your site is in good health and is not vulnerable to attack. To make sure you have all your bases covered when it comes to external services the technology card has as list for reference with the most common services that you can check off as to supplement.

Search Engine Optimization:

Back in the good old days to the web, you could trick the search engines into giving your website higher preference for writing your web code, a certain way and adding extra bits of information on your site. Those days long gone and today it is the content itself and how that content is shared that makes a big difference. Search is still important but distribution is quickly going beyond this old method of judgment content. So focusing on optimizing your site for sharing should be your first main concern. Luckily much of this split optimization also improve your ranking on search engines and in most cases it has more to do with good writing than it have to do with tinkering with code. On technology card there is a list presentation the technical basics of sharing and search engine optimization and how effective each of these are? These technical elements joint with planned writing will help you get your content found shared and click. Let's take a closer look; a regular blog post consists of three main elements the title, the contents and taxonomies. Many polls also have fourth optional elements in the form of images. All these play into how your content is shared and how it's indexed on search engines; if you only have your regular title and irregular content here's what will happen. When it is shared, all social media the title will be picked up and displayed in the title field in the preview; below that the expressive field demonstrates the first pair of sentences of your article. What happens in search engines depends on what brand of look for the user made. Title of the polls will be the title in the search results; but the explanation is either being the first fastens of sentence or it will be a sentence that matches the search results exactly. This last part is important to know; if you want people to find your content on specific searches, make sure those searches are in fact spell out in your posts that way Google and Bing can match them exactly. For search, the title and the page content is of medium value; but for share they are both of little value; because these fields are shortened and pulls titles and intros are rarely written with sharing in mind. That's where the meta-title and description fields come in. The Meta Title and explanation will only be visible in search engine results and when the content is shared on social media that means you can modify these fields to make the content more findable and shareable. When filling these fields out keep in mind that their short so put the most important information first; if the original post title was how massive court save thousands on installing solar panels, the meta-title should be solar panels saves thousands. The description should be short and should ask and answer a question and be expressive of the content of the post; all in 160 characters or less; tricky but it can be done. The third element is taxonomy or group and tags; though these have only medium impact on search there's still important and here's why? When search engines index your site, the use a spider script by crawls through your entire site following every hyperlink they can find; that means if you set up a smart taxonomy structure and organize your content while Google will index your content based on the structure and this will in turn make your content easier to find. There is no tricks here; simply good organization so categorize and tag post and you'll see a small return; When it comes to images thereto main elements that matter: the featured image and image alt attribute. The featured image option usually standard and blogging platforms. In your blog this usually means the image appears as a thumbnail on index pages and the same is true when you're post is share on social media. In the polls preview on Facebook and Google plus you see the title the explanation and the featured image. If you don't select the featured image these services will find a random image on the page and use that instead and that doesn't always work out the way you wanted to. The image alt attribute is an overlooked element that can have a great impact on search ranking. The alt attribute is the alternative description of the image displayed if the image is not displayed. This text gets indexed by search engines meaning if you set applicable information about the posts and the image in the alt attributes, searches on Google will shorten the image. For example; if I was a retailer for Bombay cloth Ltd and I posted my photo on my blog with the alt attribute set to Maharstra Cloth Ltd only people searching for my name would discover that image; but if I set the alt feature to Bombay cloth retailer searching for Bombay reailer would see my face in image search. Simple and effective; just remember that the alt attribute is a explanation of the image, if you start putting other in sequence in there and spent that is not related to Google police will come and get you. Share and search optimization is more of a good strategy that it is about technology; by writing share friendly meta titles and descriptions systematizing your content while designing a featured image in setting descriptive alt attributes, you boost your blog's online with minimal effort.

Content:

You've now reached the content creation stage; here you find the content card. The content card will help direct you through this procedure. In the goals strategy and technology cards, you can now start the process of creating a content strategy for the blog by asking for key questions. What are we aiming to do Google blog? How are we doing this on the web? Who in arraign and how do we measure success? The answers to these questions laid out on the goals and strategy cards; it will be the framework for your content strategy. With this in mind you can start creation decision about the content strategy? In creating a content strategy is to define a niche for your blog and from there define key topics to cover in assigned those topics to content managers and contributors. Finding the niche for your blog can be a difficult task but it can also be used as a tool to clearly define what sets your business and its know-how apart from the rivalry. To start the process you need to define where you think your company strengths lie in terms of expertise; because this is where the expertise says this should be the niche focus on the blog. The next step is to research your competition; do they have a blog or social media presence? what really talking about? Are the providing valuable information about the industry? What they are not talking about? For an green energy industry, it may turn out that rather than sharing information about solar energy itself something all the competitors are doing, the niche lies in the data green energy industry has collected over the years about how solar energy is improve the overall productivity of the clients or how it has changed the public or internal perceptions and that case, the niche would be how to improve overall business performance and public perceptions through the use of green technologies. Now you need to search the web to see who else allocation in order about the same niche is. If there is lots of information out there already, you need to refine or redefine your niche and searches. In the end, you have a clearly defined area of expertise but you can excel at without having too much competition. Within these defined you can move on to define key topics; here I would advise you to pick no more than five subjects or categories to be addressed. This will further refine your content making and give arrangement to the blog. To refine these key topics, you can used phases like the Google ad words keyword tool which shows you what type of keywords and phrases people are searching for on Google. For green energy industry, these topics could be solar savings, green initiatives, public awareness, education and the like. When you define these topics marked them down on the content card and assign them to a content management.

Types:

Before you start producing content, it's important to consider what content formats and what types of content you want to publish on web. Let's look at formats first; bold web is text based. You can also publish images, videos and audio on the web with great achievement. Making a choice about what formats you want to publish both of launch and also down the road will make the planning and setup of the blog easier and will also allow you to allocate the necessary funds to make each content format victorious. The most basic content format is text and it's also the easiest format to create as the web is text; you have to publish the text and it will be found indexed shared and spread throughout the web. You can tweet your text to be better indexed more easily shared and more compelling to the visitor but the overall production of text is straight forward. Images have been important all the web and continue to be so; by using images intentionally in content either on their own or in a gallery or as illustration elements in your posts, you increase the value of your content. Just remember that when you publish images on the web you have to have a license to publish them; but apply the correct title an alternate description tags to the images so they are indexed properly. Video is quickly becoming as important as text on the web and for good reason. Properly produced an informative video content is easier to digest than text and images and requires less work on the part of the viewer. The disadvantage to video is that it is hard to index as the web doesn't really understand the content in a video file. If this videos is being a part of your content plan, you need to allocate funds for proper video production including good audio tools and containment & you also need to consider transcribing all your videos into text to be published alongside your videos for better indexing. Audio has been around on the web for a long time and it's having a resurgence today; thanks to new sharing platforms. Depending on the type of business your company is in, launching a podcast fundamentally a downloadable radio illustrate on the web can be beneficial; however like video, audio files require production funds in transcription to be the most effective. Cyber only prioritize this content format, if it is directly related to your products. The content card shows you the different content formats; checkoff options you wish to focus on. With your formats defined the next step is to decide what types of content you want to produce. Different types of content have different impacts and can reach different goals and audiences. Be focus on one or two types of onset and refine the strategy and then implements more types down the road, when the blog is well-established. Let's look at some general content types; the most general content type on a business blog is the news item, which is just like the name proposes is communication about news and events in the company; while this may be interesting for stakeholders and customers waiting for new products, the news content type has little social and interactive value. Other types of content can have more of an impacts; Q&A posts tips & tricks class and conversation pieces tend to get shared more and also generate discussion and contribution and if you really want to start a conversation and place yourself in the debates, opinion pieces can be effective as long as the view are in line with the business goals and philosophy. My recommendation is to start with news items and two or three of the lively types, tips & tricks, tutorials or discussion. This way you'll be able to share news about the business and also provide content the guest will want to interact on web, find useful and shareable. Check off the content types you want to focus on the entire content card. Once these types are well-established in the blog has some grip, you can assign capital to start publishing more content formats and more content types.

Contributor:

Depending on the content strategy and how the business blog will be structured, you need to have one or more people vigorously create content for the blog. People are referred to as contributors; one common challenge and running a business blog is to find the people to be contributors and also get them to actively contribute. The key in making contributors is possession and actions; make the contributors take ownership of the content on the blog & feel like their assistance are part of the job identity. You should also engage with the contributors to give self-assurance additional aid. In your business there will be staffers who are experts in their field and who love to share their know-how; these staffers are prime provider material and they are usually easy to convince to become contributors. Influence their skill and talent and engage them in the planning process of the blog, in particular in delineation the niche and key topic and inquire for their input on what they think would be good content to be share on the blog. By making them fraction of the team & giving them a say in what content they should produce there would be more invested in the end product. They can tell the public about what they do and also educate the public and the rest of the company. Identify a small group of key contributors distributed across the company and profile them in a big way on the blog, give them bio pages columns so they can drive people to their own content and encourage the contributors to share their content with coworkers and friends and business contacts. Once these key contributors are in place and actively causal; give confidence them to join other members of the staff to contribute as well. The key contributors can take on the role of counselor to the rest of the staff; directing them through the process of sharing their know-how in an easily digestible way. That way you'll get more staff interaction and avoid a situation where staffers feel left out. By employing this strategy, you can also produce a welcome byproduct that the executives of your company will see as a positive and that may help solidify the importance of the blog in the eyes of management. Collaborative contribution to the blog will encourage collaboration and communication within the company and trained employees to become better communicators. In this way the blog can help the employees of the company know each other; better understand each other scrolls and get a better understanding for how the company works and that my friend is a win on all fronts.

Creating:

A common question when people launch a new blog is what to write about? The answer to that question is right about what you know. This is easier for a business blog and it is for personal blogger; because the business has a specific topic and target audience and us you been following along this book you've carried out a pretty clear path for the contributors to go downward when creating content. Even so, motivation can sometimes be hard to find especially if the business you are in concerns a relatively dry topic that the general public feels is boring. Fortunately there are ways to get over the inspiration for. To get you started let me share with you some seeds of inspiration; answer questions; all business get question from clientele both existing & prospective. Each of these questions and their answers become a blog post. This answers two troubles in one. You get a blog post but at least one person will read and you published answer on the web; so that the next person who has the same question will find it on your blog. Ask questions: reach out to existing and prospective customers and asked them what they want to know more about. This is a great way to set up a list of possible prospect blog posts & it also gives you a great indication of what the company needs to put out more in order about and where the current announcement strategy is failing. Percentage as a quarry about future blog content rather than a study about the client, you also more likely to get responses you can even sweeten the deal by contributing to include a by line about the person inquiring the question and their businesses in the resulting blog post. Right tips tricks and tutorials:

If your business sells a product or service the customer would use any training on; published tips tricks and tutorials on how to use the products and not just how the customers will use it and publish tutorials about how your company employ the produce and technology. The one way do this is to ask the staffers to write tutorials about how they do belongings as if they were scripting it to themselves for later reference because this often results in more detailed and practical instructions. These types tutorials are popular on the web and can be a great source of visitors. This is also a high-quality topic to make video content; particularly if tutorials focus on computer software.

Comments on News Items:

If there's a hot topic in the news or on social media that relates to your company or its products or services, jump on it immediately; issue statements, opinion's, perspective and facts that contribute to the conversation, while at the same time pointing to the company expertise in the field. Here it's important to remember that these are not popular marketing pieces about your company but rather actual contributions and insights to the debates. If there valuable people will think absolutely about the business by relationship. So no marketing pitch is necessary; Quote others and contributes your own view:

Coding other blogs and online sources with proper attribution and links and then commenting on their information can be both easy and effectual. You can even add facts, figures, perspective or insight to them. The inventor of the satisfied will also turn out to be aware of your presence and be encouraged to interact with your blog. You can also leave comments on the unique blog post or source to show you're actively taking part in the conversation or simply hijacking. Creating strategies for coming up with new content is simply a matter of thinking about what you know and how you can share that with others. By using the seeds of inspiration you should be able to produce a wealth of prospect blog posts & other content lacking getting irritated that there's nothing to write about.

Images and Graphics:

Images and graphics can be employed for all from illustration to eye candy and a blog. They can even be the main content of a post or be part of the gallery. When using images correctly they can become an important part of your blog and reason for people to look your blog. Now look at images on the web; if you look at the code of a webpage, you'll see the images are actually just links but are replaced by images by the browser; that's why they referred to as put back basics. You place a link to an image in your code in the right way and the browser will find image and place it on page that means you can technically take any image from anywhere on the web and displayed on your site. I say technically as in actual life this is something you should never do. So let's answer the main inquiry first: what images you employ on your blog. The answer is you can use your own images; once you or your staff is taken once, taken by photographer, Hardware Company and you can use images you have a license to use. Any other image is unavailable & may not be used. You may get licensed images from many locations. Stock image companies like istock photo provide licenses for images in your websites; photo sharing sites such as Flicker have images released under different creative commons licenses. The Creative Commons materials can be used only under the conditions of the specific variants of the creative commons license. For business blog, the best practice scenario is to only use images either in use by or for the business. If you have an image you can add it into your blog in a variety of ways. We won't get into precisely where you should put your images in your content, instead look at how to properly add them into your content & make certain they get indexed & shared. If you add an image to a blog post, you should always apply an image title used mainly to keep track of image within the blogging application, an alternate description describing the contents of image for search engines and browsers that don't display images and when necessary a caption with photographer links, information and other precious information. This ensures that images indexed by search engines and information in the image is communicated to the followers even if the image is not displayed. The alternate description of an image may be applied subsequently these standards; if the image contains information the text should describe the image. If the image is a link, the text should give details the target of the link and if the image is for decoration and has no informational value the alt attribute should be left empty. The images and videos card has information about proper image markup and how to use all tied for quick reference. You should also consider setting the most important or descriptive image as the featured image. This will be displayed alongside the title and description of the post and search engine results and when it's shared on social media networks. Using images in a blog post the right way can come into view boring at first but previously a system is install place it becomes easy and impacts of a great image is well worth the effort.

Videos:

Video is quickly becoming as important as text on the web and with good reason; videos are easy to digest and take less effort to watch then reading an article. They can also be entertaining and informative in a way no written article can. On the disadvantage side videos are costly to produce and it's challenging to make them appealing to the audience. If you have the resources and talents to make videos work they can easily become the most important marketing and communication asset in your overall strategy. Unlike text and images, publishing video online require specialized infrastructure. You can simply put a video file on the server and embedded on a page and be done with; video files are large complex entities that require robust server technology and the correct formats and players to work and to add to the complication we have a myriad of platforms from web browsers to tablets to smart phones, all with their own code and players to take in consideration. Combine, this is a perfect storm of complexity; fortunately this is not something we have to worry about because others have done all the work for us; whether you want your videos to be public and shareable or private and restricted, their services that will do that either for free or for a small fee. If you want to go the free roots in your publishing videos mainly to reach as many people as possible, YouTube is another great service. You may get the widest accomplish & younger people actually use YouTube as a search engine to get an added assistance that way; on the disadvantage side YouTube is besieged with ads and links to other videos from other people and YouTube comments need to be monitored closely; but all this can be managed to a degree. If share ability and final distribution is what you once YouTube is the place to be. If you want to control your video not have any advertising or only have advertising you control or you want to restrict access to only select viewers, there are plenty of other options available; value mentioning is videopress Viddler & brightcove. All these are for paid video hosting providers that give you complete control of the contents. The downside is these videos do not distribute as easily and are less likely to give you the possible for viral sharing; regardless of the platform you use when you publish a video online you have to maintain a few belongings in mind. Always offer a descriptive video title to ensure people find the video when they're looking for content on the subject matter. Consider providing a full text transcript of each video in the video description and too in the blog post you implant the video in. This'll make it easier for search engines to find the videos. If you're using YouTube or female add tags and proper descriptions to ensure people find your videos and other indexed properly. Moderate comments were turned off altogether; you do not want the underbelly of YouTube to embarrass on any page with your business name on it and finally remember that as with images, you need to own or have a permit to use any video imagery or music attributed in your videos. The images and videos card has a quick reference show to how to obtain your videos indexed on search engines.

Implementation:
Design:

You've now come to the implementation stage; this is where all you've done so far comes together and you make decisions on how to build the blog itself. One important element to consider when launching a business blog is how to make the blog fit in with overall an online visual identity of the company? When a visitor lands on the blog she should immediately recognize it as part of and belonging to the company. This can be done through the inclusion of logos, colors and fonts and this can also be done through layout and customization. Depending on how much your company is willing to invest in the blog and is the sign, there are several levels of customization that can be done. Of course the preferred approach is a fully customized blog that looks and feels exactly like the company website and is integrated seamlessly; when taking this approach it's important to keep in mind that the nature of a blog is quite different from a normal business website. You have to design around elements in the blog but don't currently exist in the website. In other words some redesigning is required even if you aim to match the blog to the company website. If your company has a style guide this document should be the basis of the blog design. A redesign of this magnitude is not always realistic; at least not in the beginning stages of the blog project. Even so, bringing in a designer specializing in business blog design and your chosen blogging platform is a sound investment. If you're working on a shoestring budget, you can still ensure the visual identity is carried over by following some basic guidelines and thinking about your content and a smart way. The most important element that must be included in the blog design is the company logo and name. This should be appended with the word blog or some other signifier to make it clear the visitor is now all the blog and not the main website. Next you must provide a link or links to the main website preferably in the main menu. A common solution is to add a button from the blog on the main menu of the main website and then copy elements of that menu over to the blog. That means the majority of menu buttons on the blog will be pointing to the main website to have to get creative with placement of blog specific menu items. This can be solved with careful planning. Another option is to have two menus one for the main website and a second one that only shows up on blog pages. This ensure separation between two elements but it's also more complicated to implement. If your company identity includes key colors or color schemes incorporate them in the blog as well. That goes for background colors, separator colors, link colors and so on. A good place to use key colors and a blog is in the background of layout elements like the header, sidebar and footer you can also include them in other ways. The key here again is to be created. Visual identity can also be attributed through the use of fonts and font layouts; to make an effort to match the font family font size font kerning and line spacing between the company website and the blog. In addition to designing the blog to share of visual identity with the main website and the company, you also have to consider how to incorporate blog specific elements in a graceful manner. Chief among these elements or social sharing buttons and comments. There are many options available here before business blog; it's important to use clean unobtrusive and professional looking elements and use them sparingly. Finally all blogs and websites published on the web today should be mobile friendly that means ensuring that the blog is responsive or that there is a mobile option built-in. Most blogging platforms have both responsive templates and mobile options available and they can usually be configured to fit with your visual identity. The easiest way to ensure your blog is mobile ready is to test it on mobile devices like tablets and smart phones and ensuring the blog is easy to use across these devices. If not you need to change your settings; spend more time with the design to make it work properly.

Publish:

With goals and strategies in place, technologies picked out, content creators lined up and the design completed, you have everything you need to start the job of setting up and publishing the blog. To get you up and on your way you may have some tips. First off, create all lot of content before you publish to blog I recommend to the extent that 60 posts to be estranged into two groups of 30; one for backdated posts; one for future schedule posts. Before you make the blog public, published a 30 backdated posts and spread them over a reasonable time. Anywhere from 3 to 6 months or more. If you have an existing blog or online magazine and you want to move the contents over to the new blog make sure to back date in the published material to the original publishing dates. This way when visitors come to your site there is an documentation of content they can find the way through. A blog with only a few entries is unimpressive and gives a bad feeling. It may be argued that backdating blog posts is insincere, but I'd counter that by saying you're merely backdating the posts to ensure that the easier to digest for the visitor. A large number of posts published on the same day is confusing for the visitor and makes for poor navigation. The 25 future schedule posts should also be entered into the system and scheduled to be released on certain days and times; that way even if you leave the blog to run on its own, new content will be published for a period of time after launch. This step is important to ensure you don't launch a blog only to have no content on its. By preparing and scheduling content you give yourself the content team time to get used to the new situation of having to publish content on an ongoing basis. I also recommend having 10 to 15 Posts in the system but are stored as drafts. These posts are to be used as fallbacks for when no new content is available; this is a safety valve to ensure continuous publication even when things are getting in the way of blogging. Before setting a date for the launch of the blog, set aside time for extensive user testing. Make the blog public to the staff in your company and have them test the site and use all its functions. By having people outside the blogging staff testing the blog you'll be alerted to anything that is not as it should be, from confusing navigation to buttons and links that the work and these can be addressed before the launch. In preparation for the launch, contact key stakeholders and industry bloggers to let them know that the blog is going to go online shortly. You can also give the restricted access to the blog ahead of time to peak their interest. Set the blog up in its final location well ahead of the launch to ensure all assets work properly to avoid anyone accidentally visiting the blog ahead of time you can employ to maintenance mode plug-in or module but hides it from the outside world and finally launched a blog in the middle of the night several hours before the official launch. This gives you time to fix any last-minute issues and deal with them without having eager visitors trying to use the blog if something goes wrong. When launching a blog for business you have to assume some things will go wrong. Being prepared with existing contents, extensive beta testing and a preemptive launch; you can minimize the effect of any issues with the blog goes live to the web. The implementation card has a checklist with all these steps you can use as you prepare for the blog launch, only when all items are checked are you ready to take your blogging life to the web.

Blog Schedule:

One of the reasons why blogs are so effective as marketing tools and why search engines like them so much is because they constantly have new content; but also means if your blog isn't publishing content on an ongoing basis its level of interest will drop and drop quickly. One of the key elements of professional blogging and that's what a business blog is all about is to publish content on a schedule. If content is published on a schedule, visitors and search engines alike; will come to expect new content interest will rise accordingly. Just think of it in newspaper terms, if the newspaper came out only sporadically and at random times, you go through the trouble of picking up a copy. Before the blog is launched sitdown with the content team and contributors and work out a schedule. Schedule should have two levels: thematic days and contributors. To make the process of planning content for the blog easier thematic days should be defined and set; as an example you can say that everyone stay the blog will publish a Q&A article and every Friday the blog will publish tutorial. That way the content team will be able to climb content for future weeks and the visitors will note to come back on certain days for new content. At launch, the blog should not have more than two such predefined days. Setting up thematic days doesn't mean you can only publish content on both days or that the content must fall under those themes. Quite the contrary, these days are buffers; to ensure content is being produced. They should be interspersed with other content whenever it is available. That said I recommend restricting publishing all the blog to most onetime per day for the first several months. Blogging fatigue will kick in at some point and if the publishing schedule is too aggressive off the top that fatigue will kick in long before the blog has to foothold it needs; both internally and in the public eye. With thematic days to find you should also make a schedule for the contributors; for each of the thematic days in the next several months a contributor should be assigned; a topic or title should be defined. That way everyone involved knows what the responsibilities and deadlines are and what is coming down the pipeline. Any posts that fall outside of the thematic days should also be schedule and assign properly to ensure publishing distribution and other content team has bandwidth to handle the incoming content. To provide a apparent impression of what is experiencing with the blog it's a good idea to create a shared calendar that all involved parties have access too; that way everyone can see what is plan what is currently in the works and when new content will be published.

Interaction:

Getting your blog posts shared on social media is a great way of carrying in new readers and starting a discussion about your company and your brand. To make this happen, you have to ensure your content is shareable and also worth sharing. The trick is to customize the message to the medium; let's take a look at some best practices on how to get your content out to social media once it's published and also how to keep the conversation going and encourage further sharing. Assuming your company how social media channels like Twitter handle, a Facebook page and a Google plus page set up, the first thing you should do when publishing a new polls is per stuck post out through these channels. The temptation here is to set up an automated system but blust posts out all the channels at once using a boxed message; but this is not an effective strategy. Twitter, Facebook, google plus and other social media channels are all very different and all have their own languages. Customizing the message for each channel will make a big difference in how people interact with it. For twitter the key is to say something that will catch people's interest and also encourage them to share or re-tweet the message; because twitter only gives you 140 characters and your URL will take up a good portion of these, it's important to be concise descriptive and appealing; that usually means reframing the polls title into a question or conversational statement. While something like did you know solar energy can make your company cool; read more at link can sound a bit hokey; it's far more effective than simply saying new post and in the title of the post. For Facebook and Google plus a longer conversational posts is to be preferred. When posting the link ad some extra information or perspective and provide a brief summary of the posts without giving away all the details. The idea here is to catch the reader's interest in an environment where people expect you to be conversational and then drive them to the blog for more detailed analysis. What interesting about Facebook and Google plus is that many people don't actually read articles the like plus one or share; they just read the post itself along with a description. If the first person who sees your article does not read it she might share it with some friends who will. On Facebook and Google plus you can also use images to further booster the attention your post will get. This requires a bit of planning and a great picture; usually with some text on it; can be extremely effective. In this scenario you make the image the focal point for the descriptive text pointing to the article in the image description. If the image is appealing, it is likely to be shared even if people don't know there is a link appended to it and the more shares you get the higher the likelihood of someone clicking on the link and going to your blog. The best combination here is the mix of regular link posts, an image link posts in equal measure. For twitter, it can also be a good idea to post the link several times throughout the day or the week to reach more people. This is also true for Facebook and Google plus but on a longer timescale. One supposes to share. It's important to interact with anyone common thing or sharing on the polls to show your making them part of the conversation.

CHAPTER: 8
DIGITAL MARKETING RESEARCH

Consumers and companies leave large amount of valuable data all over the web. Digital marketing research is the process of harvesting the data and putting it to good use and that this Book is all about. In this section, I like to share with you how you can conduct your own digital marketing research. We will discuss how to employ big online data ecosystems to research consumers and competitors that may be use free tools to carry out the research but also share with you a few premium tools used by professional marketers. Once you will familiar with the research techniques, we will provide you with a live example of a recent challenge for which you conform the solution which are else not visible in marketing research.

Research Ethics:

Important consideration before proceeding with online research physical considerations require that the applicable it's perfectly acceptable to use transparent online research tools together more conduct about consumers and contenders. There are several belongings that would not be considered as ethical; for example hacking a competitor's website; gaining unlawful access to data is not ethical; interviewing competitor employee in false pretenses is not ethical. Creating and publishing generalizations based on qualitative opinions of article on unconfirmed data and identified bloggers would be un-ethical. Accessing data which is not publicly available certainly not ethical.

Unethical Practices
- Hacking a competitor's website;
- Gaining unlawful access to data;
- Interviewing a competitor's employees under false pretenses;
- Creating and publishing generalizations based on the qualitative opinions of unconfirmed data;
- Using nonpublic data.

Always keep these things in mind when carrying out market research. Something to imagine about before we continue would you be Would you be happy if your competitor used the same research strategy as you, or would you feel that your privacy was violated? You feel that your privacy has been violated. However, we will go doing our research in a more ethical fashion.

Largest Online Eco-System:

In this section, we will learn about the largest online ecosystem on web. This will enable us to collect more representative investigate samples which will augment the correctness of our research and enable better decision making power. You can use the free version off of Alexa.com to tell you about the largest ecosystems in the world.

You can customize this by country, or by category. Let's go to Browse Top Sites and let's imagine you're in the United Kingdom and you'd like to see the biggest websites in your country then just go to country scroll down to the United Kingdom and that we go. Here is a list of the biggest websites in the United Kingdom salted by the amount of traffic they receive. More specifically, you can got health and women health etc.

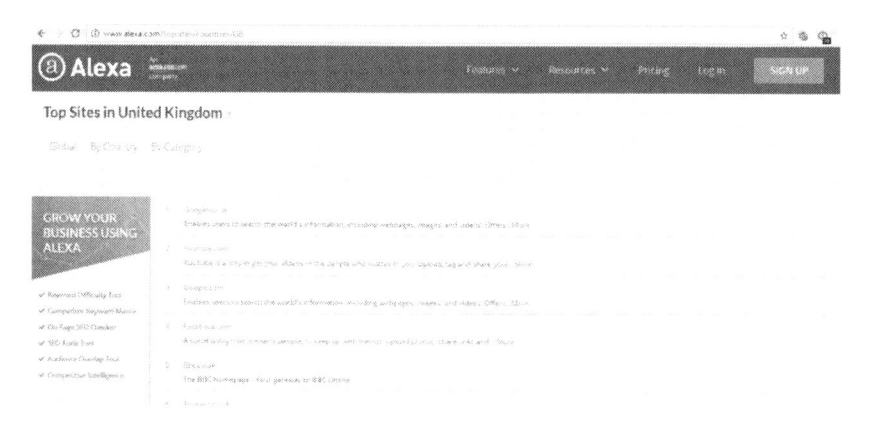

Let's imagine the during the health business you click on health let's be more specific door in the women's health category you click on women's health and there we go it salts out the biggest online ecosystems but relates to women's health in the United Kingdom.

But let's have a look at the ecosystems that can be particularly helpful with our research. We will discourse the first ecosystem is Google. It is useful to us because in most countries represents the largest part of the population online search requirements. Therefore when we use quantitative research to establish public demand, we will use the Google keyword tool.

Google
- Keyword tool
- Webmaster tools
- AdWords

Amazon
- Customer reviews
- Best-seller lists

Facebook
- Ad inventory
- Consumer sentiment

Linkedin
- Customer reviews
- Best-seller lists

The second ecosystems Amazon is useful because in most countries represents the largest part of the population online shopping habits. Therefore, when we use qualitative research to understand what consumers such as women think of a product and why bolted that we can scrape Amazon reviews and analyzes them . The third ecosystem was Facebook. In most countries Facebook represents the largest social media network. Therefore we can use quantitative research to evaluate Facebook's advertising inventory which will tell us the size of online interest groups, all branded communities etc. Facebook has become more sophisticated in the sense that it is also enable us to carry out a mixture of qualitative and quantitative research for example how many repeat buyers offset the products exist in a brand community. Third one is linkedin which is become the world's most popular social network.

Linkedin was perhaps the most useful tool for B2B research and for services for example physical products mainly retail Amazon which attracts reviews but where services are involved, recommendations and endorsements, Linkedin can serve as a valuable alternative to what Amazon offers at the same time.

The Web Constantly Evolves

We can crack down key influencers in various industries around the world by using Linkedin. Remember since the web is constantly evolving you should keep track of any rising online ecosystems and for this you can use Alexa.com this tool shows you which are the biggest websites globally and also bought country.

Quantitative Vs Qualitative research:

Now we're going to learn about all types of online research. Before we get started try to imagine what exactly these that you want to know about a product, a company competitor.

Start with a question:
What exactly do you wish to know about a product, market, or competitor?
Then:
Choose the best research method.

This will then enable you to decide which type of research would be best to use. Let's look at the two types of research; firstly there is quantitative research here we will measure data and statistics which will reveal the numerical body for example how many visitors or how many web pages or how many monthly web searches.

Quantitative Research:
- How many monthly visitors?
- How many webpages?
- How many web searches?

Think of "numbers"

Qualitative Research:
- Why and how?
- What color?
- What style? Think of "details.

    Secondly there is qualitative research where there would seem to understand how many rather go for analyzing why. For example consumer reviews can tell us why people favor a certain product over another; or how they arrived at a decision to buy the preferred product. It is useful for digital marketer to know about both qualitative and quantitative research methods.

Both Method Can be useful

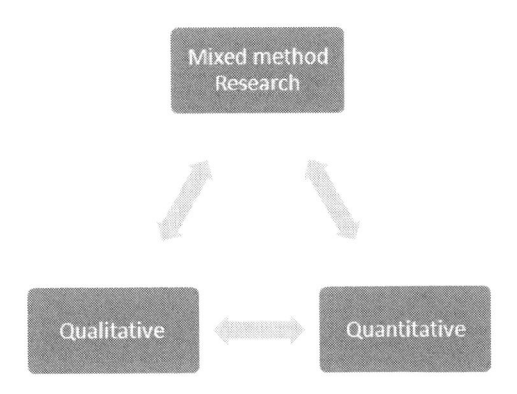

```
        Mixed method
          Research
         /        \
        ↙          ↘
   Qualitative ⇄ Quantitative
```

    The finance manager may want to understand how much should it cost to generate a more through at the energetic; then we would use quantitative research to find out how many consumer search for a product and how much Google charges for the relevant advertising inventory. On the other hand let's imagine that the development manager wants to know ways to improve the next public release; then we would use qualitative research to find out what consumers disliked about their existing product, what consumers like about the competitor's product and then absent features that consumers want. Then we also use a combination of qualitative and quantitative research which is typically referred to as mixed method research.

How to conduct Ethical Research:

So how can digital marketing research help you in your career or the business we work? In a few moments I will walk you through why? It is such useful skills to list. Firstly, when we look at the area of consumer research, before investing huge amounts things like product expansion or content marketing, we can actually measure consumer demand through quantitative research which will give reason for the next steps that we require to take enough strategy. Before wrote about the possibilities of online investigate, we can even utilize it to get better prospect products or services; for example by analyzing quality feedback from one online consumer reviews or by sharing it with our research and development team.

Consumer Research
• Measure consumer demand - quantitative research
• Better strategic decisions
• Product development - qualitative research

Secondly, we can also do opponent research. Can you think of any business today which does not have competition? To become a alarming contestant, it engages so much more than simply copying good-looking websites. We need to know a lot more; for example how many pages or content the website has; what is the approximate traffic sources and more importantly what a fruitful investment would be required to compete on equal terms.

Competitor Research
• Goes beyond website aesthetics
• Website metrics: ages, visitor levels, and traffic sources
• Overall comparison of competitor landscape

The ability to provide this sort of research to a number of websites can provide us with an overall view of the competitive landscape. Consequently, the aptitude to perform digital marketing research constraints how business intelligence influences the strategic decisions that we make. Fortunately, consumers leave launch collective and individual digital footprints on the web which is valuable to digital marketers. For competitors, there is a sign that they can run but they can't hide because research can tell us so much about the completion. Yes there are infinite areas of research that could be of interest but to provide you with a solid foundation, this book will focus on the following. Firstly, in our introduction to online research will cover qualitative and quantitative research will become acquainted with the largest online ecosystems where researchers gathered and discussed some of the research limitations.

Then, in research on consumer demand will learn practical tips on how to measure consumer demand through online ecosystems like Google, Facebook and Amazon. Next, we will look at research on the competition. Here, we will learn how to use Google and LinkedIn to research the competition. Finally, we will put knowledge into action; where we will provide solution in the forms of a case study to demonstrate how effectual study can be carried out. To bring to a close, digital marketing research enables us to gather useful information about patrons and contestant which can be used for better decision-making.

Tools of Marketing Research:

So far we focused on using free of charge tools that you could use to study the competition in the market. I am going to show you what professional marketers would use. There are a lot of premium tools that makes the marketing research easier.

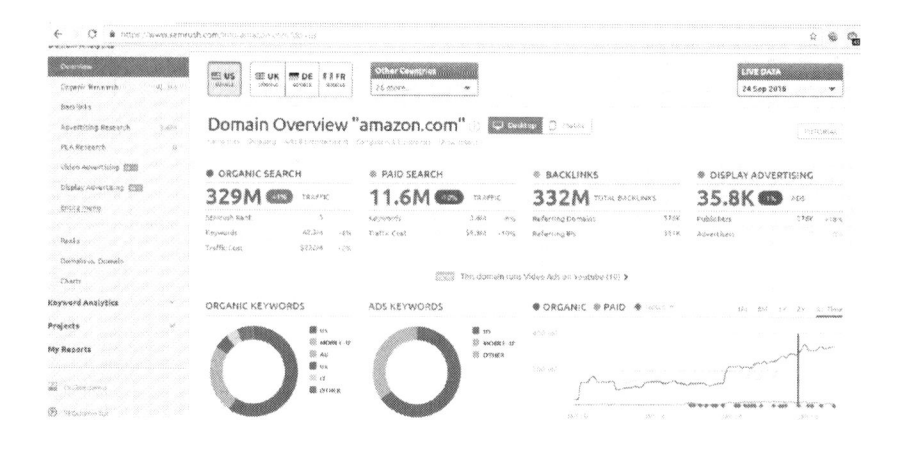

The first one we going to use is called https://www.semrush.com/ and let's just imagine that we would like to research something to do with the online shopping industry in the United States or we will use the website for amazon.com was our example hit the Enter and let's see what it can tell us about for amazon.com and its competitors if we look at amazon.com semrush estimates that the organic search traffic is about 329 million visitors per month.It estimates that about buying Google traffic all of the paid search traffic that equal to about 11.6milion visitors per month. It also tells us that it estimates that there is roughly 332million back links coming into amazon.com. But if we scroll down it has been estimated off the amount of mobile visitors there and it also tells us the top organic keywords that are being searched for full visitors who go to draw amazon.com.

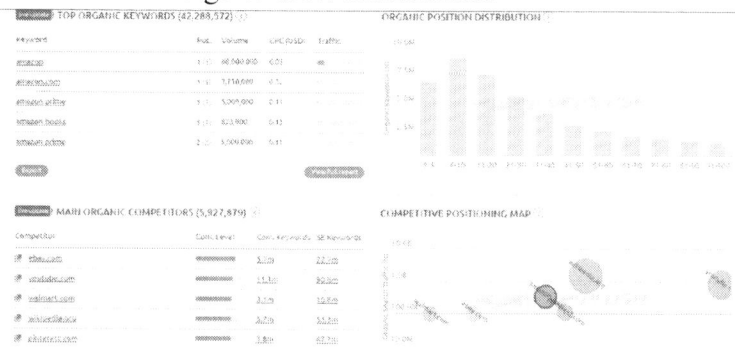

All in one Digital Marketing

This is pretty useful because if we wanted to compete with amazon.com we would have an idea of how much it would cost us to compete. It is also helps us to estimate the cost per click to compete. It is similar to Google keyword research tool. something else that is interesting here is the way in which competitors all displayed we can see that some of the competitors for provocative commentaries like ebay.com walmart.com, and so forth it goes a step further and shows the professional marketer and competitive positioning map which shows us some of the key differences that it has with competitors. This is really useful if you're trying to plan the new marketing combined to spot gaps in the market. What else we can find semrush.com is interesting here is that 19% approximately is Branded traffic. So it is people who know about amazon.com list searching specifically for provocative, and about 81% of the traffic all probably searching for other keywords. We also see the top paid keywords that for amazon.com. We can even see here that other competitors are competing quite ferociously with amazon.com by traffic. We can see here that ebay.com walmart.com competing previously.

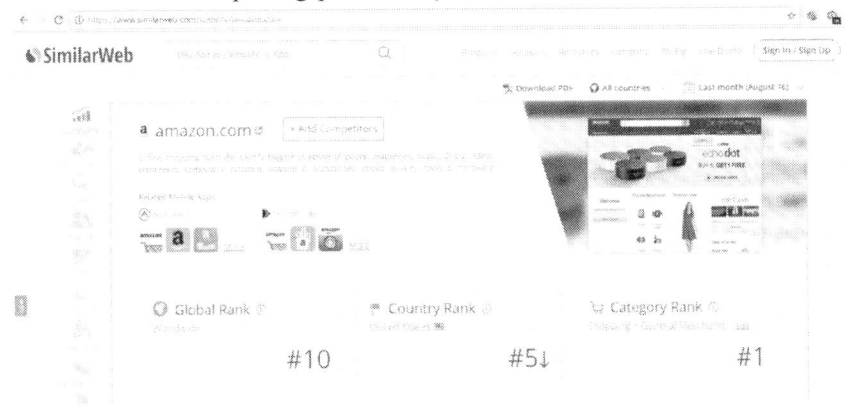

Let's open up another tool that we can use which is called compete.com and similarweb.com and will use the same example of amazon.com no similar web will bring up a silent estimates and what is interesting here is that the estimates of monthly visits on similar web is quite different than what we've seen on compete.com. This just goes to show that the research is never 100% accurate and there would be variances. The interesting metric that we can see here besides the amount of visits is the amount of time spent on the website and this is a good metric to look at. Because the time spend on the website shows us the extent to which the visitor would regard this to be good quality content. If the bounce rate was much higher the visitors perhaps not find what they were looking for. If you scroll down to the various other bits of information that is useful to choose which countries the visitors originated from. Chooses the traffic sources here we can see that amazon office to strong brand because most of its graphic is direct traffic (**42.45%**). In other words people knew about this website a fairly. A high percentage of the traffic is referral i.e. 23.21% which also indicates that for amazon may have quite a high referrers i.e. affiliate marketing process. Almost 25% of the traffic come from google search or from other search engines.

We can learn from some of the websites on the main referrers to draw amazon.com and among them http://slickdeals.net/ is one of the main. Since this is the free version, we do not have information about all websites here. But it is suggesting that there is another 995 websites such as slickdeals.net, referring traffic to amazon.com and also see the destination sites of where visitors go off. As we scroll down, this provides us with more information about the search traffic it tells us about the organic keywords that people search for as well as the paid keywords that can tell us which of the social media websites all the most prominent first we can see Facebook is taking the lead they with Youtube. It also tells us wait for AMAZON is likely to be spending its advertising budget it suggests that facebook.com and https://www.techbargains.com/ are the top paid advertisers. It also measures the ad networks through which the ads all distributed and it suggesting here that the Amazon Ad system is the leader followed by intent Ziff Davis out brain.

So forth it also attempts to profile the visitors by telling us which interest category they belong to. It also provides us with a preview of websites that are very similar to amazon.com such as ebay.com. What is also interesting on similarweb.com is it will provide us with details of apps that are related to amazon it's got details off apps on the Google place store.

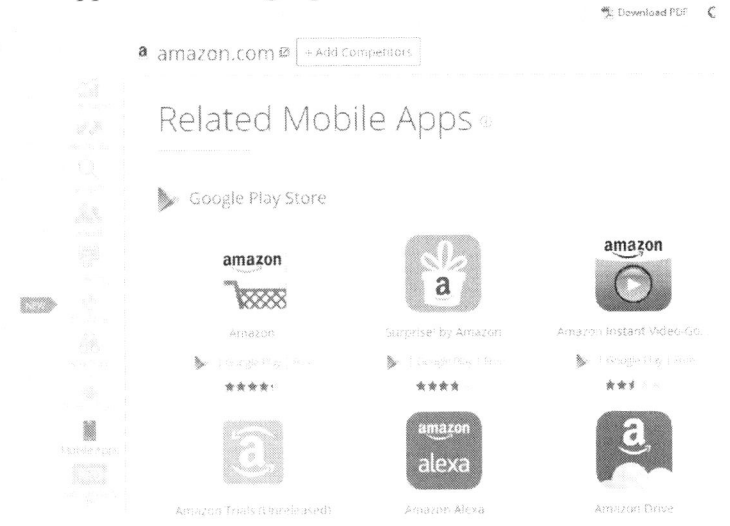

If you click on the tab it can provide us with more details. You can add competitor on sismilarweb.com to compare the details of the website details which is really helpful for people.

Challenge:

Now we're going to review our knowledge with a challenge and the solution. This will be a fun and you can repeat this as many times as you like and even use different examples when you repeat this. So, here is the confront: Fund's director would like to understand more about the potential cost and effort required by retailers who sell a book in the United Kingdom but he wants to know about business that employ their own websites rather than third party websites such as Amazon.

Challenge: Water Filters UK
1. What is the scarch demand across the country?
2. What is the monthly cost of targeting 10% of search demand (paid search)?
3. How many pages of content required?
4. What are the other notable competitors?

      They would like to know the following four questions. Number one is that what the approximate search demand is across the country; number two is what would be the monthly cost of targeting approximately 15% of the search traffic through paid search numbers free how many pages will be required to compete with the most prominent Google competitor for organic search traffic. Number four is which other websites all considered to be notable competitors in the market. Think about these four questions and when you're ready these proceed to the next video.

Limitation of Digital Marketing Research:

      My research is ever not 100% accurate. In any research there are usually limitations and digital marketing research certainly no exception because of many reasons; fro which why accuracy can be affected. Let's just blame a few of them: Firsstly, cultural differences. Some cultures are very open and discussed almost anything on social media. On the other hand, some are less open and people to express themselves the Republican. This makes it harder to generalize our findings on the global scale which consider regional and regulatory limitations. Facebook and Google represents the sentiment of many people around the world but in countries like China and Russia other solutions are currently in place. Market share can also vary if you're using Google to determine the market demand is worth noting. Google's market share your country could be different. For example the UK Google is almost 85% of the market share but in the USA it has about

70%. The high of the market share, the more accurate way they can represent the data that we produce. Then, it's also worth noting that off-line inquiries and phone sections are not recorded online. Conventional trading is very much alive still there is full. Therefore, online demand doesn't demand total demand for a product. If 1 million people searched for an item online, they may well be another million people didn't use the item But physically went to a stole the search for their product equally.

Research Accuracy Factors
- Culture differences
- Regional and regulatory limitations
- Market share varies
- Offline transactions not considered

It is useful to point out to stakeholders that the findings of our research are approximate and indicative without claiming 100% accuracy. It is something for you to think about what factors all likely to affect the accuracy of your research? At work what of the ecosystems that you will use for measurement. These are very good questions to ask before getting started.

[Be Honest with Stakeholders
What factors can affect the accuracy of your research at work?]

As you can see conducting digital marketing research can give you access to all sorts of data and insight about her customers and competitors. These data can help you make informed decisions to grow your business and reach even more customers. You like to learn more about digital marketing research. There are a few resources and I recommend firstly explore the analytics. Be sure to check out the Google analytics that gives you detailed look at how you can use Google analytics to uncover insights about your company.

Solution of the challenge:

Now we going to provide a solution to these four questions and draw up a report of fact. Firstly, we head over to the Google adwords and we click on **tools>keyword** planner and we scroll down to '**get search volume data and trends**' and make sure that your filtering reflect one of these that we searching for United Kingdom. So it's targeting the United Kingdom and we start off by entering our most commonly searched for keyword or at least just into the keyword that you think people will be searching for most commonly. In our case it is book and we scroll down to ***Get Search Volume.*** The tool instantly return the results and in this case we can see that there is an average monthly search volume of 110,000 searches for this particular keyword the competition is quite high but this does not represent the total volume because people might actually search for other search terms that we don't know someone going to look a little further to see what else they could be searching for. The head over to tools again to keyword planner and click on search for new keywords using the phrase website for category. And enter book make sure it fit to the United Kingdom only and we click on get ideas. and when we click on add group ideas will see that there is mainly search terms that are frequently being used. in here you can select the ones that we think on the most relevant to our product and really learn more about how the consumers think and what sort of questions they're asking when they search we can select the relevant ones and export the data onto an Excel sheet. we can actually remove the relevant data retain only what is the most relevant and then at them up to see what is the total search volume really that there is available so you can take this data you can click on download get it in the CSV file and then start sorting through the data now we simply use the data from a spreadsheet to calculate the approximate cost of acquiring 15% the monthly search traffic in this case when we use book our calculations suggest that the 15% off the UK search market every month willing to spend around $7081 management did find this quite useful but may actually decide to approve and 14,000 over budget in order to talk to 30% of the market. Remember that your findings may vary depending on the keywords that you decided. Now we move onto the next phase of our research, we going to check the competitor's website to see how many pages they are indexed in Google so we simply write site:amazon.com on book to document which is the main competitor we click on Google search and Google indicates that there is roughly 9,96,00,000 pages that are indexed for amazon both Mac. So we know that in order to compete with this website for organic search results will need to create the least amount of pages finally to find out who the most prominent competitors all according to Google were going to use another search string and we going to write relates to how long water filters document it into and Google will show us 1, 52,00,000 r results of websites that you consider to be very similar.

Final Steps

Analyse data → Draw conclusions → Create a report

To how once we carried out the individual parts of our research and balance of the questions we can follow this simple three-step process whereby we would *analyze the data* to consider what is relevant when we drove on to reason from the data and finally were able to control the **findings** together and **produce a report** that all the stakeholders may find useful.

Using Amazon to measure Demand:

Using Amazon to measure the demand and to measure

consumer sentiment is quite easy. However, Amazon does not provide us with specific tools that can produce inside the consumer searched item. Amazon does not reveal what items consumers couldn't find. However the items that were found and were purchased offer us with many pointers both in terms of qualitative and quantitative research. The easiest way to get started with Amazon is to have a look at the bestseller lists inside Amazon.

Just go to Google and just type Amazon bestsellers and click on the link that will take you to amazon best seller website and now you console which are the department that you want to look at.

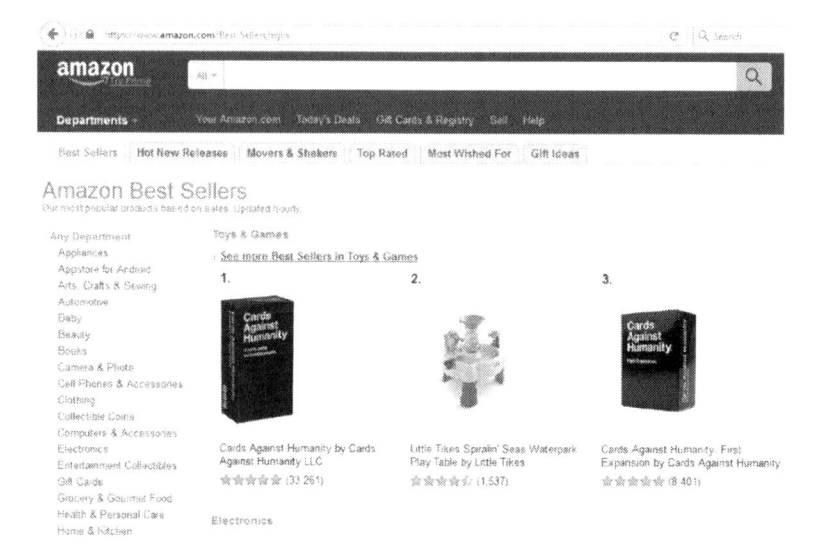

Now go to head over to the Electronics department and see what we can find as you can see at the point of doing this research will to Fire Tablet seems to have been very much Demand in United States. Fujifilm Instax Mini Instant Film was also in the moment. But there is so much more that they can be gather from Amazon. It is easy to use this tool in order to research consumer sentiment this can be done by scraping and analyzing consumer reviews. Average prices can be measured and if we know the wholesale price of the products. It is even possible to estimate the profit margins. Species scraping technology may gather feedback and qualitative data presented to us in the spreadsheet will enable us to take our time and analyze the data and learn more about what consumers think about certain products. You may be pleased to know that Amazon is not the only shopping ecosystem that we can scrape data from this commend him for any other website for example eBay.

Using Facebook:

Facebook is the world's most prominent social media platform. However we must remember that it does not have a leaving share of search market. Therefore Facebook, show us how many people searching for any particular field.

However, they are other useful indicators which we can find when we use Facebook as a research tool. For example whether there is a strong society support for fastidious brands or products. Here we can go to measure things like Facebook likes, number of followers etc. We could look at qualitative consumer research assists such as consumer sentiment. Here we can go to monitor the feedback and reviews across Facebook that we can find. We also look at consumer behavior related to online purchases that is because Facebook permits us to talk with visitors according to their online purchase behavior as in the library. You will find very extensive resources to help you most of the Facebook marketing environment. The insights produced by Facebook are different to that of Google. You may still find it useful to complement your research that was sold to think any competitive product see if you can find interesting conversations about them on Facebook tried to assess the level of support for their brand also see how it relates to your own portable services.

Using Google:

In Countries where Google represents the majority of the online search market, it is one of the best tools to measure the demand. Google enables advertisers to measure the demand through a free tool called the *Google keyword planner* which is available to anyone who's got the Google adwords account. The Google keyword planner can promise all sorts of attractive data, for example how many monthly searches for a specific term or the relate to terms people searching for. It can also show us of data for particular country and global data. Now let's look at how to use the Google keyword planner which we will find once we looked into a Google adwords account. Under the tools go to *gets search volume data and trends* that we can simply enter the keywords that we want to know more about so let's imagine we were a hotel group and widowed hotel in New Delhi, India and Mumbai but also interested to know about the market amount for hotels and other cities so we go ahead and went into each of these keywords. Now scroll down we click on get search volume and within seconds you will provide us with some interesting information we see from the results that. Hotels various about 673,000 searches per month for hotels 1,300 searches per month for hotels in Mumbai and 260 searches per month for hotels in New Delhi. It is a great start but it is not conclusive because we can learn so much more. To see what else we may go to Google keyword planner we going to hit to a different category; search for new keywords using a phrase website and now we enter the keywords again hotels in New Delhi, Hotels in Mumbai and Hotels. Google will present us with some interesting information under two headings it will give us at Ad Group Ideas and keywords ideas. Under ad group ideas we will see groups of search phrases that will very similar to main idea which authentically synonyms to be a regional keyword all related items. when we look at the volume of data Google provides us with we realize that the initial hotels in Delhi or

Mumbai represents just a fraction of the searches that reflects the total hotel demands. Other Keywords such as Hotel last, hotels booking also stands for higher volume of data. Here's a tip for you if you were want to do in-depth market research, it gather together all the relevant results that Google provides us with on this page will added to the spreadsheet and sort out them to find which is the most relevant to your regional idea and find the combined total that give you the total amount of keywords ideas. Google will automatically display individual keyword searches that all really related to your regional ideas. and sometimes when we add up to some of the low volume of keywords to give a second far exceeds the volume of the original key phrase that we used. So we want to remain open-minded in our research as to what we might learn and how we might benefit from that. Another useful feature is that with Google we can access data applicable specifically to certain countries so I'm the targeting options you may want to choose just one country; for example how many people living and while searching for a hotel in New Delhi. So repeating this individually can also tell us way in the wool of biggest amount laws for specific product and if you think about it we can lend very specific things such as local search phrases to people in India such differently than people in from us before they book a hotel in Boston. people often surprised the first on the axis searching search from Google. I encourage you to try this out yourself just remember that the market share Google has seen no specific country will of course affect the accuracy of your research. The bigger the market share is passing in any country, the more representative our research will be of the overall population.

Using Google AdWords to measure the competition:

Google keywords can tell us a lot about how competitive markets all in different countries and industries. In most cases there is a direct correlation between the indicative cost per click that the market this prepare to pay and the market competition.

Level of Competition	Correlation
Often reflected in cost-per-click (CPC), although approach to lifetime value can influence CPC	CPC: level of competition? *Exceptions apply

However, there can be exceptions in some industries the lifetime value of the customer is much higher and for that reason even with little competition companies are willing to pay a lot additional per click. For example, the University that sells a three year degree program would value students total spin at approximately $70,000 over three years and it would be willing to pay around $25 per click to attract students. The college on the other hand that sells one day Excel course would value the students initial spin to be perhaps $100 and might be another hundred and $50 over the next three years. Here it might be willing to play a maximum of only $0.25 to $.45 per click to attract the students.

Now let's look at how to measure the competition for these keywords by using Google's free tools. So we had over the Google ad words now and in the tool section on the keyword planner we go to the gets search volume data and trends. Now we are going to enter the keywords that the university students all likely to search for and the college students and will compare the two. University students are likely to search for an IT degree or MBA in information technology where is the college students are probably going to search for an Excel course or IT short courses. Now scroll down and just click on the get search volume. Google tells us that for an Excel course there might be 590 searches per month and for IT degree course 1900 and so it also indicates that for shorter courses, a customer might have a shorter lifetime and value cost much cheaper. Excel course would be 3.75 but an IT degree which is a much longer course there is a high volume of the student and it will cost 31 pounds per click. The same goes for the other examples that we used. We should try to use these insights to make better decisions an example of how an excellent researcher would do this is if you could find internal company data to present management with evidence that the users of the Excel course want be proven tools approaches IT degree of the later course. In this case you could actually avoid competing on the more expensive keyword such as IT degree and focus on selling an Excel course first off to which you would upsell IT degree to the same users thereby avoiding completely to compete on the more expensive keywords. Remember that research is only the beginning how we interpret the findings of the actions that we take it.

Google Search String to find the completion:

In this lesson were going to research the competition of using the few Google search phrases to inquire specific information. Let's imagine you're starting a new website and it will be important to know where the competition is? What is the position in the market? If you are able to find out a few things about the competition's website and online market, what is it that you would like to note? We may propose three questions; firstly we going to laws how many website pages do they have? We may want to list media and affiliate websites linking to the website. You might also want to ask how many similar competing websites already exist.

Questions about Competitor Websites

- How many website pages?
- What is the list of media and affiliate websites linking to the website?
- How many similar, or competing, websites already exist?

For example, we do use free well-known search strings on Google for the first question we will simply say **site: Trevago.com**; the second question **link: Trafalgar.com** and for third question **relate: Trevago.com.** Let's head over to Google and see what this would look like. we enter **site: Trevago.com** and click on enter button and Google suggests that there is roughly one and half million pages on the domain **Trevago.com** now if we enter **link: Trevago.com** and hit the search button Google tell us that they are all roughly 130 free websites that are linking to **link: Trevago.com.** Now moving on to the next question we will simply say relates: **Trevago.com** and click on search button and Google will show us that they know other websites that are closely related to **Trevago.com.** Please note that when you're using Google search strings you have to be specific they should focus for example you say site: **Trevago.com** holding one line this will work correctly however easy say site with a space for **Trevago.com** it will not work equally easy say site: with the space **Trevago.com** this will not work.

No Spaces or "www."

site:trivago.com **(will work correctly)**

site trivago.com **(will not work)**

site www.trivago.com **(will not work)**

There are of course many good-looking aggregators that the present the same information as Google. It will be appearing on fancy dashboards and so forth and I'm certainly fascinated by fancy looking – as it is costly. These are premium tools some of these tools include some of the semrush.com and you can see that the free version provides us with an aggregate and it will show was the entire website that the related to hotel.com. Google search can help us in digital marketing research but would encourage you to go onto Google and try this yourself with other examples.

Using LinkedIn to measure the competition:

In the B2B and services world, Linkedin can tell us so much about the competition. It also help us to track down great talent when we are improving our human resources. Sometimes we won't understand that the competitors strategies and regaring the strategies, we don't know simply how they achieve their aims. These things can be better understood when we know more about people that the company hires and Linkedin is all about people. But let's imagine that your business brainpower unit would prefer to supervise opponent closely. You're interested to know what sort of talent they hire and how do they actually perform their existing tactical games. Let's go to company California water system and we find the company's corporate page on Linkedin. Then we can regularly visit LinkedIn to see what's office listed under the business and how it altered. We can also supervise the different cities in order to understand the direction in which the company is expanding we can even have a look at how they recruit abroad in order to know which countries they are going to expand.

There is a lot more we can do is LinkedIn let's look at what other options they're all available. We can use the link in sales navigator to help us develop better B2B relationships. The strategy can in fact become automated and completely data-driven because of the tools Linkedin provide you with. It is also use Linkedin system to follow competitors and you can use this to analyze the key influencers to know what they think. You can do a lot more with Linkedin than simply research. You can become a thought leader on Linkedin and release information that other people can find useful in their conducting that research.

This book explore the tools and methods of digital marketing using social media such as facebook, twitter, blogging and email marketing. The more you precise and acquainted with these tools, the more you will enjoy these tools

****

Made in the USA
Middletown, DE
06 November 2016